Also by Angee Barcus

Snapshots Of Lisa: A Candid Look At Down Syndrome And Snippets Of Lisa's Life

Loving And Learning: Life With Lisa And Down Syndrome

Mountains To Climb

Lisa And Down Syndrome Challenges

Mountains To Climb

Copyright © 2018 by Angela Barcus All rights reserved.

No part of this book may be reproduced or used in any form without written permission from the author. The only exception is by a reviewer, who may quote short excerpts in a review.

Printed in the United States of America

ISBN-13: 978-0-9973832-3-2

Dedication

To Lisa, who has weathered many storms and climbed many obstacles to get where she is today. She has helped me to see the world in a different light.

To my other children, Tammy, Brent and Adam. You have been a big help with the book, giving your input about certain stories. Lisa has always had your love and support and that has helped her to be who she is today.

To my husband, Monte. With your help in reading and editing this book, you have made it better because of your keen insight. You gave me a different look at the stories from your perspective. I did not realize you saw things differently during some of the trying times.

Thank you all for being you and for helping me throughout this journey. It has been a wonderful experience for me.

Acknowledgements

To all of you who have been a part of the proofreading and editing, I say thank you. You know who you are, and I am forever grateful that you wholeheartedly agreed to spend some of your precious time helping me. I couldn't have done it without your help.

To my husband and children, all I can say is thank you for listening to my never-ending comments about this book while I wrote it. A special thank you to Tammy and Joe, who willingly agreed to write their story about Lisa for this book. Your expressiveness and honesty helps to complete this book in such an extraordinary way.

Mountains to Climb

Several years ago our "little Lisa" was born,
Changing hopes and dreams,
'cause she's not of the 'norm'.
Her birth brought happiness….and tears,
Lost hope for the future, and many new fears.

How could we cope, how could this be?
We wanted the best that she could be.
And now we know this still can be true,
Though we've had to adjust a dream or two.
We've gone through many good and bad times;
Many roads to travel, many mountains to climb.

Her first ear infection made the ER's day.
Her first surgery took my sleep away.
Her first rollover from front to back,
Had us all on the floor where we could clap.

She made some slow but steady strides,
Like sitting, crawling, walking
and piggyback rides.
I look at her now and wonder about us.
We were mad, scared, uncertain.
Oh, why all the fuss?

Her achievements are many,
we're as proud as can be.
She seems just---SO NORMAL;
did we doubt it could be?

I have faith in the present
and the future holds hope,
That she will live with society
and our family can cope…
With the questions, the problems,
the hopes and fears,
That will be with us daily
and all through the years.

I thank God that we have her,
and all she can do.
She has shown us that life
need not always be blue;
Behind the dark clouds…a silver lining or two,
By how we adjust to the different and new.

Angee Barcus 1987

Table of Contents

x   Preface

P. 1   Lisa's First Apartment

P. 15   Special Olympics

P. 25   Police Academy

P. 33   Lisa And Boyfriends

P. 39   Tattoos

P. 43   Ears Pierced Again

P. 49   Plays And Talent Shows

P. 55   National Self-Advocate Convention

P. 67   Thank Goodness For Lisa

P. 75   Anecdotes

P. 85   Technology Talents

P. 97   Going To The Doctor

P. 107   Sjogren's Syndrome

P. 113   Thyroid

P. 121   CPAP

P. 127 Eating And Exercise

P. 135 Voices And Depression

P. 145 Medical Record Keeping

P. 155 Vehicles

P. 163 Preferred Lifestyle Plan, BASIS And Letter Of Intent

P. 169 Special Needs Trust And ABLE Accounts

P. 175 Useful Information On Benefits And Assistance Programs

P. 185 Church, Spred And Reach

P. 195 A New Apartment

P. 207 Lisa Speaking Out

P. 213 Looking Through My Glasses

P. 221 The Visitor

Preface

Mountains To Climb: Lisa And Down Syndrome Challenges is about Lisa's adult years and the challenges she faced. There are a few articles on her health issues and I reveal the unexpected and unknown health problems that Lisa has had to experience. We did not realize all the scenarios that could occur and I am sure doctors did not tell us all that they knew, because each child with Down syndrome has their own specific health issues.

I also write about Lisa and her personal life; her dating, having outside interests in the community and finding that one special partner. I share stories about Lisa and her interests in self-advocacy and speaking out for others, which brought back memories of when she was quiet and shy. That is no longer the case.

In sharing this third book with others, I am also including some of the resources that we were able to utilize to help Lisa with her medical and financial needs. I mention local, state and national programs and share general information that will help others as they weave through a maze of confusion in the quest to get services. I am just a parent of a child with Down syndrome and I don't know all the answers. I hope the general information gives others a place to start when searching for answers.

I never dreamed that I would ever finish or publish one book, let alone three. Once I got started, I discovered there was enough interest and that I had plenty of personal information and stories about Lisa that could be useful to others. I appreciate all my readers who have given me tremendous feedback. I appreciate all those who encouraged me along the way during this process and those who gave me help and direction when I was gathering specific information on difficult topics. My belief is that others will benefit from what I have shared about our experiences and that the stories about Lisa are encouraging. I recall a saying that, with any luck, fits what I have tried to accomplish. "You can't pass through this world without affecting someone else." I hope I have made a difference.

Enjoy the book, and thanks for reading!

Lisa's First Apartment

Lisa kept asking about moving into her own apartment. She was finishing up her second year at a community living program and would be turning twenty-one. She still lived at home and I thought things were pretty well established in her daily and weekly routine. She attended the community living program each day during the week, learning how to live on her own. She learned to cook, clean, get groceries and money management. She learned how to plan, organize and schedule appointments. She improved and added new social skills. She had assistance with community involvement, as well as support when preparing for job interviews as she worked towards getting a job. She spent several hours a day trying out different work places, so she and the staff could help her when deciding what job she liked and what job she would be good at when she was ready to try working in the community.

In the late afternoons and evenings, she had activities with friends, and she had in-home support from a local organization that would take Lisa out if she needed to go shopping or to just get out for an hour or two with other adults. That in-home program offered many supports for Lisa. They helped Lisa with housekeeping, meal preparations, grocery shopping and running errands. They would also help Lisa with medication reminders, local transportation and companionship if necessary. Lisa needed some of those supports while she was still living with us, but the most helpful was just having someone take her out as a companion.

This local organization helped Lisa to gain greater independence as well as supporting her daily needs. The services were available to Lisa while she still lived at home. Lisa met with this person at least once a week and they always did something different. It got Lisa out of the house and gave her new experiences to try with someone other than a family member. It was a great help to us, as Lisa's dad and I both worked and that left Lisa home alone at certain times. The staff person Lisa had matched well with Lisa's personality. This person was very friendly, courteous and supportive of Lisa, and her likes, wants and needs. They got along well. Some days they would go for a walk. Other times they would go have a soda. And, once or twice this staff person took Lisa to get a haircut. This was a great way for Lisa to learn how to do things with other people, and not always have to have her mom or dad take her places and do things with her. We had to start letting others be a part of her life, working with her and helping her to become self-sufficient and able to live on her own.

We finally started to seriously look for an apartment for Lisa, not knowing how it would work out or where to start. Lisa, her dad and I went and viewed several apartments together, but never really saw anything appropriate. At least, not from my point of view. The process of looking was long and disappointing. We ended up buying a duplex, with the idea that when Lisa was ready to move out, one of the renters might also be ready to move out. I thought that would be ideal. To have one side of the duplex for Lisa and ask the renter of the other half to help her, to watch out for Lisa and take part in helping Lisa when she needed something. I even thought we could give the renter a break in the cost of rent, to encourage the renter to see that this option wasn't such a bad deal. That didn't happen the way we planned. The duplex we bought had two good renters and neither one had any notions of moving. So, we had lost some time waiting for a renter to leave and Lisa was getting anxious to start living in her own apartment. Maybe she didn't like our rules, and was just ready to move on. Whatever the case, we started to look at apartments again. That's when we heard about Section 8 housing which provides housing assistance for people with low incomes.

Section 8 housing stems from the Section 8 of the Housing Act of 1937, according to Wikipedia. The site reports that the Housing Act "authorizes the payment of rental housing assistance to private landlords on behalf of approximately 4.8 million low-income households, as of 2008." [1] In Lisa's case, it helps her by paying a part of her rent. We helped Lisa with the initial application and later on with the six-month and yearly updates that are required to ensure that Lisa continued to qualify to receive benefits from this program. The yearly form was quite long and it had numerous questions on different subjects. The questions asked about income, expenses, who might be living in the apartment setting and other pertinent information the agency needed to make an informed decision on how much Lisa needed to pay for rent in the coming year. Lisa's rent seems to stay close to the same amount each year, varying slightly dependent on her finances. The program subsidized the difference between what she can afford, according to her expenses and income, and what the rent actually is. Meaning, she got a break in the cost of her rent.

An inspection was done each year by the Housing Authority agency, which I welcomed because they always found issues that needed attention. In the past, there have been broken door handles, sinks that leaked, a sliding door off its' hinges or rollers and appliance issues. The apartment complex maintained the units well, but if the apartment management isn't told of any problems they must assume that all was ok. It's nice to have someone other than myself or Lisa's dad do a walk-through to check on things, as they can go through and thoroughly check for all the possible problems.

In finding out about Section 8 Housing, it also saved us a lot of time because we basically stayed with those apartments that were a part of the Housing Authority list of possible rentals available. We started with an apartment complex that was within 15 minutes, (walking time) from our house. It took us all of three minutes or so to drive there, so that was handy. We didn't consciously choose something close, but it was the first one on the list that looked like it might be a good fit for Lisa. And, I guess it was, because she has been in that same complex ever since she moved out of our house. Over the years, about 16 years in fact, Lisa has lived in three different units there and they have always been just what she needed and a good fit for her living arrangements.

Her first move was to a one-bedroom apartment on the first floor of a building that had a total of eight units. At first, I thought I might like her on the second floor, because I was concerned that if she had her living room and bedroom windows on the ground level, it would be too easy for robbers or strangers to access. Silly me. As it turned out, she took a ground floor apartment and it came to be a good choice. She had some difficulties with managing stairs and that was the only way to access the second floor units. Also, being on the ground floor made it easier for Lisa to watch for her bus ride every day. Since she would no longer be at home, she had to get set up with a door-to-door bus service that was provided by the city for a nominal monthly fee.

We secured the apartment unit with a down payment and began to make plans for the big move. She had already bought some bedroom furniture a few years earlier, so that was one expense we didn't have to worry about. She didn't have a lot of money, so we tried to find items that were less expensive or free. The "free" would be items from our house that we no longer used or had an excess of, such as bath towels, linens, blankets, kitchen towels and so on. She did end up buying some bedroom items, including a new bedspread and curtains that were red; her color choice. For the kitchen, she received some great gifts from the family, including some big red, heart-shaped bowls, a juicer, a dip maker, a frying pan, a coffee maker, a hot dog maker and a bagel toaster. Little did I know that one of the best purchases we made was a George Foreman Grill. This kitchen appliance is easy to use and you can cook lots of items on it. Lisa used it mainly for meats and I guess she became a pro at using the grill. It's also easy to clean and I felt it was safer for her to use instead of the stovetop for cooking. I believe this was and still is a 'must have' for Lisa.

Lisa thought she should have a shoe organizer in her bedroom closet, so she bought that item. The apartment gave her a choice of bringing in her own washer and dryer or they would supply those appliances and she would then pay for the cable bill instead. I guess the apartment complex offered one perk or the other, but not both. Lisa didn't own a washer and dryer and we weren't too keen on buying a set for her, so we decided that Lisa could pay for the cable and use the apartment complex washer and dryer. That quandary worked out well.

She picked out a couch, chair, end tables and lamps to buy, and within a short amount of time she was ready. She already knew how to do her own laundry and since the apartment unit she was in had a washer and dryer, she wouldn't have to haul all her laundry to a commercial Laundromat. I tried to go over how to rinse dirty dishes, how to load them in the dishwasher and how to clean up the kitchen after cooking, which involved wiping the counters and sink. And, the community living program helped Lisa to refine and build on a variety of skills that she first learned at home. It was all the basics that we should all know how to do when we think we are ready to leave the safety and comforts of our parents' home. Before Lisa moved in, we even practiced having her lock and unlock her apartment door, because it was a little tricky at first, having to turn the key just right and jiggle the handle a little. But she got it.

We spent weeks hauling items to the apartment whenever we had time to take a load or two over there. We arranged the dishes and food in the cupboards, the furniture in her bedroom and living room and the clothes in her closet. I was surprised at how the rooms, closets, cupboards and drawers filled up quickly with stuff. But, it was all Lisa's stuff and that was good. She was excited to finally have this new chapter in her life begin. But me, not so much. I knew she could live on her own, but I worried about all kinds of things. (And guess what…most of those worries never came to fruition.)

The day finally came when I took Lisa over to her apartment. All her belongings were there and she wanted to be there, too. So, one Friday after she got off work and after she had supper with us, I drove her to her new home. I had packed an overnight bag for me, because we had discussed the issue of me staying the first night with her, and she was agreeable. That is until we parked the car right in front of her unit. She looked at her sliding glass doors that gave a view into her living room and then she looked at me. By the way she looked at me, I thought she might not want to stay there at all. But I was wrong. I think her apprehensive look was due to the fact that she didn't know how to tell me what she was thinking. Slowly, she said "Mom, I want to stay here by myself tonight. I will be okay." What??? I was packed and I was ready to sleep on the couch. For a moment, I was sure that she might have even wanted to go back to her old room at our house. Yet what she was really trying to say is that she was ready to be on her own. Of course, this is what we had wanted for years; for her to be independent, for her to move on, to live in a place she could call her own. And, all of a sudden it was time. So, I gave her a hug or two, waited while she got her things out of the car and watched her walk the few short steps to her front door. She didn't turn around and wave. She just opened the large door to the building and walked in. I sat there, wondering when I should drive away. Did she get her door unlocked? Did she lock it once she got inside? Yup, the living room light was on so I knew she got in. But why didn't I drive away? Well, it's because I couldn't. I was crying. As usual.

When I got home, I anxiously waited for Lisa to call. She finally called, late in the evening, after 10:00. She wanted to know if she had any snacks at her apartment. I tried to remember what foods we put in the cupboards and the refrigerator, but didn't think snacks made it on the list. So, I told her I didn't think so. I also mentioned to her that maybe she shouldn't call after 10 p.m., because that would just give me a fright. (I went into more detail about late night calling after she did it again a few weeks later.) I woke up the next morning wondering how her evening went, so I called her. She didn't answer. Well, I figured she was probably in the bathroom or cooking in the kitchen, so I waited a few minutes and then I called again. Still no answer. I wasn't sure what to do next, so I waited awhile and then decided I'd better go over there to see if she was all right. We had a spare key, so I took that with me, just in case. It was now about two hours since my first call that morning, and when I got there I rang her doorbell and waited for her to come to the door. She was at the door rather quickly and seemed glad to see me. I asked her if she checked the peephole that was in the door and she said no. So, of course I had to remind her about checking it because she shouldn't open the door to just anyone who knocks or rings the bell. Lisa said, "I know, Mom. But I knew it was you. And, I am not tall enough to look through that peephole." Which was true!

I then asked her why she didn't answer the phone. She said she wasn't home at the time and hadn't had time to call me back. Of course, I had to know where she went first thing in the morning, and she gladly told me. "I walked over to the grocery store to get some snacks." Now, here was my grown up, independent daughter being so…grown up and independent. The store was about five to six blocks away, and she would have had to cross a busy street, by herself. She reassured me that she used the light to cross, and was very careful. And, the fact that she walked there and back was a novelty, because she usually didn't like to walk very far to go anywhere. But, I guess the draw for Lisa was that she COULD walk there, by herself, and buy whatever she wanted. And she did.

There was another time when she called on July 5th and asked if I had heard the fireworks. We talked about the noise for a minute then Lisa asked me if she was strong. Well, I didn't know if she meant physically or mentally. Nevertheless, my answer would have been the same, yes you are. I wasn't sure where this question was coming from at the time, but later, when I hung up and reviewed why she might have asked that, I decided that it might have something to do with the fireworks. The noise might have woken her and she became scared or unsure of what the noise might have been. But, she must have worked her way through it, because when we talked she sounded perfectly fine. I am sure she didn't want to be afraid and she just wanted reassurance from me about her being strong

I must say, being in her own apartment was great for her. She learned to cook more, using a George Foreman to grill meats and she could make mashed potatoes from a box mix. She made lots of microwave meals, especially frozen entrees for suppertime. She tried scrambled eggs in a pan on the stove but decided that microwaving scrambled eggs was just as good and easier for her to do. And, she did a great job when using the microwave for scrambled eggs. She would scramble them in a microwave safe, glass bowl then nuke them for about 45 seconds to a minute. Then she might have to stir them a little and repeat the cooking another 30 seconds or so. I think she did a great job cooking eggs this way and I knew she would not go hungry.

We set up a doorbell that worked using a battery for a power source. This way she would be able hear when someone stopped by. Just a knock on the door was sometimes not loud enough for Lisa to hear. I set up a schedule for her (I love schedules and lists) so she could see when she should shower, do laundry, and other chores such as vacuuming, sweeping the floor, or to go with staff on outings with others. She really didn't pay attention to my list or schedule, so at some point I quit pushing my habits onto her independence.

I thought I had taught her everything she needed to know in order to live in her own apartment, but I discovered I missed an important chore; cleaning the bathroom toilet. It's not a chore I like to do, but somebody has to, right? Well, I bought Lisa a scrub brush, some toilet bowl cleaner and a base to set the brush in after using it. I tried to cover all that was important and hoped she would get the hang of it. She did not look too thrilled when I gave her the brush and told her to repeat what I had just shown her. She did well and I felt good. I have checked her bathroom on occasion, even the toilet bowl, and I must say she does a decent job of cleaning. The newest and most sensible invention is a brush that you just pop a little scrub pad onto, get it wet with the first flush and then scrub away. The bowl comes out clean, nice smelling and sparkly. Then you just pop off the scrub pad and you are done!

There was a time when I had trouble letting her live in her apartment the way she wanted. I would go over to visit her and end up suggesting that I could help her organize or clean her closets. She had a small closet near the living room area that was used for hanging up coats and storing a few items that wouldn't fit in her closet in her bedroom. Some of these items were her vacuum cleaner, broom and dustpan to use on the tile floors and shelf space for storing seasonal decorations, winter hats and gloves or any miscellaneous items that would not fit on her open shelves in the living room.

With her closet in the bedroom, I would go in, pick up clothes that Lisa had left on the floor and ask her if it was clean or dirty. Depending on the answer, I either had her put it in her clothes hamper or I hung it up. I also straightened all her clothes that were hung up but somewhat haphazardly drooping in all sorts of ways on the wire hangers. Some visits I spent nearly an hour keeping busy straightening her clothes. And somehow, I'd move from closets to dresser drawers, where I would fold a lot of t-shirts and all the time Lisa would just watch. I would ask her if she wore a certain shirt and if she had trouble answering, I asked if she wanted to give away or keep the shirt in question. I tried to thin out her collection of t-shirts because she really didn't have a lot of drawer space.

As far as other cleaning situations, I would check her dishwasher on occasion to be sure she had loaded the dishes correctly and reminded her to use the dishwasher soap when she had a full load. I also checked her sinks and counters in the kitchen and bathroom, instructing her on the importance of getting those things clean so there wouldn't be dirty areas that might be a health concern. Lisa did a fair job of keeping the place clean as far as I could see, and she never had a visit from the health department, so that has to be a positive note. I probably did more than I should have, but over time I relaxed my obsessions about her apartment and that was probably the best thing I could do for both of us.

Once Lisa got settled and in a routine at her apartment, she didn't want to go out of town with us as often as before, she didn't want to leave her place and didn't want to visit us a lot. When she did visit, she just wanted to eat and then go back to her place. She was even okay being in her apartment when the storms were bad. But, I was concerned about her, especially during one scary tornado warning. I tried to call her to see if she wanted to come over. She didn't answer her phone, so I drove over to see if she was okay. She was just fine. Silly me. She was more than just fine. She was safe, secure and satisfied with herself and where she was in her life. She was superb.

Special Olympics

"Let me win, but if I cannot win, let me be brave in the attempt."
Special Olympics oath

I am not sure when Lisa was first involved in Special Olympics, but I know she was pretty active during her grade school years. She did roller skating, bowling and swimming, and was practicing some cross country skiing before we had to move away from that first town that she called home. She tried to work hard at mastering all those sports mentioned and seemed to enjoy the time spent with friends. Once in awhile, family was also involved. I remember that one of Lisa's brothers went skating at a fundraiser that Special Olympics held. It had to do with counting laps around the rink and raising money for each lap. It was fun to watch everyone skating for prizes, and Lisa's brother walked away with a full sized waterbed. He was thrilled, and I am certain the Special Olympics organization was also, because it helped to raise money to continue to support their program and the needs of their athletes.

In the early 1960s, in the backyard of Sargent and Eunice Kennedy Shriver, Eunice held a camp called Camp Shriver to give children with intellectual disabilities a chance to discover their skills and talents. Eunice had a personal interest in this undertaking, because she had a sister, Rosemary, who had an intellectual disability. This was the beginning of the Special Olympics program being established. "Special Olympics 'provide year-round training and athletic competition in a variety of Olympic-type sports for children and adults with intellectual disabilities.' 'Special Olympics transform lives through the joy of sport, every day, everywhere. We are the world's largest sports organization for people with intellectual disabilities; with more than 4.9 million athletes in 172 countries—and over a million volunteers.' 'Through sports, our athletes are seeing themselves for their abilities, not disabilities. Their world is opened with acceptance and understanding. They become confident and empowered by their accomplishments. They are also making new friends, as part of the most inclusive community on the planet -- a global community that is growing every day.' " [2]

  I can attest to the fact that Lisa was empowered and more confident when participating in their sports. She wasn't ever really athletic, but she did try a lot of different activities over the years. I know she liked the roller-skating if she could keep to the edge of the rink. And, she had enjoyed swimming when she didn't have to put her face in the water. When she swam the width of the pool, and kept her face in the water, she usually got across in one breath. Bowling was fun for her, but she really liked the snack counter. She was always willing to try a new sport and I think she learned a lot from each endeavor.

  Because Lisa has Down syndrome, Special Olympics required her to have an x-ray to be sure it was okay for her to participate in competitive sports. The screening looks for atlantoaxial instability. According to healthychildren.org, children with Down syndrome are at a higher risk for developing this instability anomaly. Atlantoaxial instability "is caused by a combination of low tone, loose ligaments and bony changes." If there is compression of the spine, especially at the C-1 and C-2 in the neck, which is the area of concern for atlantoaxial instability, there may be serious injury if there is hyperextension or flexion at the neck or upper spine area.[3] According to the National Down Syndrome Congress, "85% of individuals with Down syndrome have no evidence of atlantoaxial instability. 13-14% show evidence of instability by x-ray only and have no symptoms. Only 1-2% have symptoms that may require treatment."[4] Lisa had an x-ray, and it revealed that her disc spaces were preserved and showed no significant abnormality. This was a good report and in my opinion, I believe there should be no further concern with this issue.

After one of our many moves to a different town and state, we discovered more sports that Special Olympics offered, but Lisa decided that she just wanted to do swimming. She did well, especially after she realized that she could indeed swim. She was in seventh grade when she felt comfortable enough to seriously compete in swimming. With help from the swim instructors, Lisa became very confident and able to swim the length of the pool with little effort. She was a strong swimmer and even though she didn't have as many years of swimming as most of the other girls on her team, she was able to keep up with the best of them. Of course, winning a medal was just the incentive to do more races, so she continued in this one sport with Special Olympics.

Once she was in high school, she had the opportunity to do a weight lifting class and she loved it. She always wanted to go lift weights at a local center and I tried to make that happen. The problem was, I didn't know much about weight lifting and Lisa's dad was still working full time, with varied hours for his work schedule. We weren't able to be consistent about the workouts, so the interest waned for a while.

About the time I was looking into weight lifting for Lisa with the Special Olympics organization, I received an email from Lisa's caseworker. She had forwarded me some information on Special Olympics that offered the powerlifting sport in our town. Perfect timing, I thought, because Lisa was asking about weight lifting, I was looking into the possibilities and here was an email telling me all about it. Of course we attended the first meeting of the season, which was at the beginning of the new calendar year, in January. Lisa was able to meet some new friends and she also discovered that a friend she had worked with at a college cafeteria was a successful Special Olympics power lifter; not just at the local and state level, but also on a national and international level as well. Knowing this young man helped Lisa feel more comfortable around these other Special Olympic power lifters, partly because she was the only female on the team at that time. Lisa rarely missed a practice and the same can be said for the meets. She tried to be at all of them. They usually occurred in May, with a metro meet and a state meet. There was a third meet that she was never able to attend, mainly because it was on a day that she worked and she didn't want to always ask for time off or miss out on her work. She was very conscientious about her work schedule. The powerlifting practices ran for about an hour, and there were always plenty of volunteers to help out with educating, observing and spotting for the lifters when they were practicing.

This group took their powerlifting seriously; they were always dressed to work out and began each practice with stretching warm-ups. They did shoulder stretches, triceps stretches, hip flexors and ham string stretches, as well as long adductor and standing stretches. They ran around the gym and tried to do jumping jacks. Lisa was not very excited about warming up, but she did occasionally try to follow what the others were doing. Lisa did tell me that she did other workouts at home using her hand weights. She loved doing curls and other flexion techniques to work her biceps, triceps and forearms. Lisa also mentioned that she would do squats at work, especially when she carried a lot of the plastic trays that were used in the restaurant where she worked. I guess if you stack a lot of them, they get pretty heavy. I'm sure I couldn't lift many.

When Lisa first started going to practice, she was very excited to be working out every week. She got even more excited when she found out that she would be able to participate in the meets. She received a singlet, which is a very tight, one piece uniform. She also got a team t-shirt, jacket and duffle bag to keep all her clothes in. Before one of her first meets, Lisa called to ask me a question about the next day's meet. She wanted to sleep in her singlet the night before, so she would be ready in the morning when it was time to leave. I reassured her that she would have time to dress in her team uniform AND eat breakfast before we had to pick her up for the drive to the meet. I don't know if she slept in the uniform or not. It looked wrinkle-free to me.

Before one meet, Lisa was trying to increase her bench weight, so she was trying extra hard during practice. That evening, she had a lot of issues, starting with the weight bench. She had trouble laying down on it, because she said it always felt so narrow for her. After moving that heavy, steel-framed padded bench, she tried again to lie down, but it was now wobbly. She stood up so volunteers could adjust the bench placement so it didn't wobble, and even though she was now visibly upset, she went to lie down again. This time it was when she was on the bench that got her upset. She was too far away from the weighted barbell, and she had to start scooting closer to the head of the bench. This was a slow process, but she finally made it and was able to do her bench press reps without any other incidents. Then her group of lifters moved on to the squats. Someone came up to Lisa and said "You're up next," and her reply was "Crap." I guess she wasn't ready for more lifting practice.

During a meet, she had help knowing where to go, how to get situated for each lift and what to do when each lift was finished. Lisa was always attentive to what was going on, watching her team members do their lifts and encouraging others that were competing. She was always a little excited and nervous before hand yet when I would be with her, making sure she had all her weight equipment and appropriate clothing, she acted pretty calm. She would even tell me, "Mom, I am as cool as a cucumber." And, she was.

After a big state meet, we ended up going out for a meal before heading home, and Lisa wore her 4 gold medals into the restaurant. She jingled and jangled all the way to the table, which seemed like a long ways away from where the hostess had greeted us. Lisa also had her team t-shirt on and her dad and I were wearing our Parent t-shirts. We were a proud group, and I think everyone knew it when they looked at us. Lisa was especially enjoying the people as they smiled when she walked by them. A similar scene happened when we stopped for gas. Again, Lisa was all decked out with her medals and her team apparel. We walked into the station to get something to drink where we had others smiling and grinning at us. I even had one parent stop and ask me a question about the event. This stranger shared with me about his own child who had a developmental/intellectual disability. It made me feel good that we could be good advertising for Special Olympics.

    A few times I would not be in town to take her to her practice, so I asked a friend of mine about taking Lisa to and from the practice. I made sure this friend knew where Lisa lived, gave her the address and a map, and then thought that having Lisa's phone number would also be helpful. I gave Lisa my friend's phone number, too, just in case. Well, the ride to and from the practice worked out great and my friend even stayed to watch the practice. It was afterwards, when Lisa arrived back at her place, when things didn't work out so well. Lisa called me to ask for help, but because I was out of town, I was of little to no help. According to Lisa, she said she arrived at her apartment and when she got inside, she realized she still had her weight belt on. This is a very important belt to wear during practice and competition, because it indirectly supports your torso, as well as reminding your core to tighten and be more rigid. Lisa's weight belt was wider in the back than in the front, and the front had a belt buckle and lots of holes in the belt to choose from. Lisa usually wore hers fairly snug, so it was tight around her waist. For Lisa, the dilemma now was trying to get the belt off. She said she tugged and pulled, but couldn't get the clasp out of the belt part. I tried to walk her through other ways, such as laying down, sucking in the stomach and then trying to unhook it. At this time, she also had a roommate, and I told her to have him try to unbuckle the belt, with her standing and lying down. None of these tactics worked. While I was trying to figure out what else to do, I hear her roommate talking to someone on the phone. He was smart enough to realize that they weren't going to be able to undo the buckle. He had called an on-call service that they both could use as part of a supported independent living arrangement with a local organization. Lisa called me back a few minutes later to say that the belt was off. After that, for me, I knew that whomever I asked to take Lisa the next time I was out of town, would be reminded to check and see that Lisa had her belt off before they dropped her off at her apartment. It was not something that I would have put on my list of possible things that could go wrong. But it did. Stuff happens!

  Lisa and I continued to do her weight-lifting workouts, even after the Special Olympics powerlifting practices were over for the season. Because Lisa was going through some mental health issues, I wanted to be sure that she had a physical outlet to help her maintain a positive, healthy attitude. I tried to spot her and she always wanted to have heavier weights put on. We would spend the hour working on more repetitions and a little lighter weight, for my sake. But, she always got a good workout and felt good about it afterwards. One time, as she was helping me to put the weights back on the rack and to wipe down the bars, she was red in the face and sweaty. But, she turned to me and said, "I love my life." I am glad Lisa found a sport that she has stuck with for quite a few years now. It gives her positive self-esteem, self-assurance, personal confidence and a true feeling of empowerment. Her determination and attitude says it all.

A few of Lisa's medals in Powerlifting

BARCUS

Police Academy

When Lisa was in high school, our local police department offered an opportunity for residents to sit in on what they called the Citizen's Academy. The brochure talked about bringing the people closer to the police department and their activities, to let them see what the police do and how it might pertain to the people of the city. Lisa was introduced to this class through her school and was highly interested in attending. The brochure gave a list of some of the topic matters, such as covering police training and procedures, as well as giving the participants a chance to speak to the police officers and ask questions. In the process, the police officers had one on one contact with people from the community and the citizens had a chance to see up close and personal just what goes on in the world of a police officer.

The class was listed to run for 5 weeks, from the 1st of December through February 24th. I thought that seemed like a big commitment, but I wasn't about to say anything because I believed Lisa wanted to attend and learn more. The sessions were in the evenings from 4:30-7:30, so it didn't interfere with any daily activities and the only evening interference was if there was a favorite show on television. But, Lisa gave up her favorite television show for five weeks because she really wanted to learn about police officers. I must add that she also started talking about wanting to *be* a police officer. Well, we talked about what types of jobs she might be able to do that are similar to being a police officer without actually becoming one. I was sure that she would not qualify for their strenuous program, for many reasons, but I would never tell her that she could not do something she really wanted to do. I always let her work through the idea on her own, and at some point she would realize the truth of the situation and shift her focus or goal accordingly.

In order to participate, Lisa had to be at least eighteen and have no history of criminal behavior. Check. She also had to pass a background check and have three local references. Check. Check. Lisa was anxious and excited when she found out that she was accepted, and I was surprised. Lisa got ready way early, which is her nature, then sat down and waited for the time when I said we would have to leave the house. She was dressed in blue, and close to the true colors of the police officer's uniform. I had given her some instructions ahead of time, just reminding her that it was set up like a classroom and that she would probably have to raise her hand, speak when spoken to and try to look at others while she was talking. As we drove to the station downtown, Lisa reviewed my instructions and made one other comment that I had forgotten I told her. She finished her recitation of the "rules" by adding, "Oh, mom. I won't volunteer for ANYTHING!"

When we were finally inside, Lisa behaved wonderfully. During introductions, I quietly asked Lisa if she was going to talk or did she want me to introduce her. She usually clams up in crowds or groups of people and this was one situation where I thought she would do just that. But, she surprised me. When she was called upon to tell the others about herself, she smartly stood up, adjusted her shirt and pants a little and then began. She had a loud voice (for her, anyway) and very good eye contact with the class instructor. She talked about Top Gun, the movie. I don't know if she ever saw it, because she was just in grade school when it first came on the big screen, but for some reason she mentioned that movie. She also talked about how she wanted to fight for self-advocates and wanted to attend the Citizen's Academy to learn about what the police actually do. She talked a lot. And I was amazed. While she was part of the audience, she listened closely to everyone else's introductions and she did not laugh, even when others did. She was very serious, listening and deciphering what they were all saying. She followed directions without hesitation, trying to listen and do just exactly what the class was instructed to do. At one point, she even received help with some of the necessary paperwork from a guy sitting next to her. She was doing everything she could to be a part of this enticing program. I was pleased and proud of Lisa and those who helped her.

The first night was introductions and some preliminary instructions. After that, the police officer in charge explained some of the current issues when it comes to policing as well as other general topics. One thing I noticed, that out of the approximately 30 people in attendance for that year's Citizen's Academy, Lisa was the only one with a disability. I wasn't surprised. There were many well-thought-out topics, and then there was other subject matter that I really didn't want to know about, but sat through because of Lisa. I suppose I could have left Lisa on her own but I wanted to be there to support her interest, and I found out that I was interested, too. The chief of police at that time talked about guns, drugs and underage drinking. Lisa was intently listening to every word. When it was time for questions she had a few, though they were not related to the topic matter. She asked things like, "When do you hire?" "What is a nightstick for?" and "What if you get shot?" One of her best questions was rather humorous though I don't think Lisa intended it to be. It was just Lisa asking a question. Her inquiry went as follows. "Do you have to wear those clothes and look like a penguin?" That got a laugh from everyone.

There was one question from the speaker, who asked, "Does anyone here want to be a police officer?" Lisa's hand shot up really fast and she had the biggest smile, grinning widely from ear to ear. The next question was, "Do you trust anyone?" Lisa was unsure about the question and had to have it restated before she could respond with "I trust my mom." There was no laughter with that comment, but a lot of people in the room nodding in agreement. And me, I was smiling. Lisa came up with the idea to bring a video recording about people she knew who had a disability to the police department, to help them understand more about disability issues. This was also received with head nodding and positive comments.

Lisa was excited when she won a drawing that was held as an icebreaker, with her prize being a t-shirt that had a photo of a policeman with some slogan under the photo. Another highlight for Lisa was going outside to see how to use a fire extinguisher. This was definitely a lesson that she was able to use later on, when she was in her own apartment. And, for some reason, during this demonstration of how to use the extinguisher, she was one of the people who used the extinguisher correctly. In her own apartment, a few years after she attended Police Academy, she and a roommate were cooking and somehow a fire started on the stove. While the roommate called 911, it was Lisa who grabbed the extinguisher, pulled the pin from the handle to be able to squeeze the lever, aimed at the base of the fire as she was taught and did a sweep pattern from side to side until the fire was out. Then, the two of them went outside to wait for the fire department. I was called later that evening, after all the excitement was over, and listened as Lisa recalled what happened, with calm and reassurance that they were ok. Wow, I was glad I didn't get the call that they had a fire in their apartment until it was all over. I was proud of Lisa for being able to remember the steps to using a fire extinguisher and immediately took action to put out the fire efficiently and quickly.

My husband attended several of the police academy sessions, and remembered that there were some skits performed that included the police officer who was in charge of this program and several people in the class who had signed up for the program. The skits were to show what an officer might have to do, like in case of a robbery or other such topics policemen have to deal with. Lisa was the volunteer for one of the skits and when it came time for her to "do her part" she was asked what would she do if the robber started to steal something. Lisa answered confidently and as if she were in control of the situation, "Shoot first and ask questions later." I am sure that this was not the correct answer, but Lisa was sure quick with her retort. At the end of the five weeks, Lisa was a part of the graduation ceremony. She was very proud of her attendance and was on cloud nine for quite awhile. Lisa worked with a friend whose parent worked at the police department, so Lisa wrote this parent a letter. On the front of the envelope, it was addressed to her friend's parent, then an additional bit of info, asking that the chief of police should also see the letter. Inside, Lisa wrote: Dear..., How are things going so far? If you get this letter can I help with the police officers? If I can, thanks. I learned how to protect my apartment and I want to be safe myself. And how do I stay in touch with the cops? Sincerely, Lisa

Lisa had a career report to write when she was still in her community transitional program. This is what she wrote:

> "A person who is a police officer may work with people or by themselves. They work at night, like a night guard patrol. They work at buildings and grounds. If you wanted to work as a security guard job you probably have to work in a small city or town. After high school, a person who is a security guard has to get training for this job, maybe by learning on the job. The lookout for jobs say that jobs in this area will be fair. This means that it may be difficult for me to get a job in this area.
>
> I could always try to be a crossing guard, border fishing game warden, sheriff, and detective or corrections officer. I got this information from the career information center. I think I would I enjoy this career. I like this report I am doing. This is fun. Even the teacher is nice. I wrote this down of what to say if you are a police officer and working with the law. 'On the floor, now. This is the police. Hands up on the car. This is a warning, a vehicle ticket. Don't come to me if you get shot or a burglar breaks into your house.'

I have a friend who is a cop. We chat about crimes, so watch out for us. We will sit on you and make you flat as a fool. So, run as fast as possible. This is the end of my report. I like taking this career class. It is fun. I like this report, too. It was so much fun to do, with or without it being homework. I really like doing this work."

Lisa had two different want ads taped to her report that had listings needing police officers. From the notes at the top of her report, it looks like she also had to follow a sheet that told of specific things that were to be in her report, like writing about the work conditions, training needed, safety hazards of the job, and sources of information, to name a few. Her oral report grade was 40 out of 40, which gave her an A+, and her written report was also A+, even though she had 4 points taken off because she didn't include a title and her form was not acceptable. The instructor had written, "Interesting report, Lisa. You have done some good research." When I read it for the first time, I was very pleased with all her hard work and how she poured her heart into this project. I gave her an A+, too!

Lisa And Boyfriends

Lisa has had boyfriends in her life, even as early as grade school. With each new classroom setting, she would mention a boy's name and say, "He's my boyfriend." Now, I don't know if that young man knew he was her boyfriend, but Lisa was very positive in her statement that she had a boyfriend. Each day after school, Lisa would mention the current boyfriend's name and tell something about him and what he did or said on that day. Lisa always got a kick out of relating the story and she seemed pleased to be able to share them with me. Most of the time, the boyfriend was someone in her Developmental Learning Program class, so I knew she was at ease with the young man because they were in the same class together.

I remember when she was in junior high, where she had a variety of regular education classes, she had a boyfriend who was in just one of her classes but I don't believe she ever really got to know him very well. He did not attend any of the special education classes Lisa took, so she only saw him in the regular education class that they had together. All I know about him is that he worked at a grocery store after school, and if Lisa and I were going out to get groceries, she wanted to go to that specific store. That was no problem for me, because I would probably have gone to that store anyway, whether Lisa had a boyfriend working there or not.

Lisa would get giddy with excitement when we entered the store, and she was immediately on the lookout for this classmate. Again, I am not sure he knew he was her boyfriend; I think it was more of a one-sided relationship. I don't think she ever approached him to say she liked him. But, as we shopped, she would look for him, and if she were lucky enough to see him, she would get shy and try to become invisible, so he wouldn't know she was there. I suppose it could even be considered a stalking situation. This didn't last long, because we didn't always go to that store and the next school year generated new names of new boyfriends.

When we finally settled in the town where Lisa attended her senior year of high school, she once again got to know some of the boys in her special education classroom. I think over the course of a year, she mentioned at least three different boys that she really liked a lot. One of these young men happened to end up at the same work place a couple years later, where they got to know each other even better, as they worked together over the next few years. I know they were good friends, because even today Lisa has some contact with him with community activities and she always seems to enjoy those times together.

Another young man was also on Lisa's radar, and they had some good times together in school. Lisa went on to a two-year transitional post high-school program, and I think he went elsewhere so they drifted apart. But, somehow or another they reconnected and sparks were flying for both of them. This was serious and I kept a watchful eye when they were together at our house. Lisa would have him over and they'd watch a television show or a movie, visiting and enjoying each other's company. Then Lisa might go to his house, and I really don't know what they did, but Lisa always sounded like they had a good time.

There was an event that happened which really surprised me. One afternoon the doorbell rang, and Lisa was the first one at the door to answer it. When I got to the door, I looked out and saw that this young man was trying to place his 3-wheeled bicycle off to the side of the sidewalk and Lisa was helping him. When that task was completed, they proudly walked into the house together. I was surprised because I didn't know that he was coming over, yet Lisa acted like she had been expecting him. So, I asked him if his parents knew that he had biked over to our house. This was when I found out that he was not living with his parents, but in his own place about a mile away. I was thinking about how he got to our house safely, because he would have had to cross several busy intersections and bike up and down some rather steep roads to get to the house.

Now I wondered what I should do. I think I had plans to be out running some errands, so I wasn't really ready for Lisa to be here and entertain him while I was gone. My next thought was to make him ride his bicycle home, but I just couldn't send him off knowing the ride home would be just as dangerous as the ride he took to get to our house. I decided I would load his bicycle into the back of our truck, (thank goodness we had the truck) and I would take him back to his place. I explained this to him and Lisa, and neither one of them were very happy. I guess I spoiled their plans. Oh, well. If Lisa had told me ahead of time of this planned visit, things might have turned out differently. As it was, I felt the punishment must fit the crime, so there would be no visiting; he was going home.

It took me awhile to lift the bike into the back of the truck. I think both Lisa and her friend helped, which made me giggle. Here they were helping, even after I spoiled their plans. They were both taking this well. Lisa and her friend said their goodbyes, shared an innocent, sweet kiss and I was ready to drive him back to his place. The end of the story? Nope. Sometime later on, Lisa got out her 4-wheeled bicycle to ride to his place. She had a 4-wheeled bicycle, because we thought that if she practiced enough riding the bike, with the two large tires that were used like training wheels situated on either side of the bike's rear tire, she would one day be able to get rid of the two large tires and just ride her bicycle as it was meant to be, with just a front and a back tire. It was a 3-speed which was just enough for Lisa.

When I got home from shopping one day, I found out Lisa had left the house without letting me know. No note, no phone call, no nothing. She wasn't in the house and the bicycle was gone. I put two and two together and realized where she had gone. I wasn't sure as to what time she had taken off, but I was sure where she was going. And, that worried me because of the traffic and busy intersections and because when she got to his place it would be just the two of them as far as I knew. Like I said, he was now living in his own place. And with the hormones raging, I wasn't sure about that situation just yet.

Off I went, taking the truck and driving over to his place to pick her up. When I got there, I did not see Lisa's bicycle and I wondered if maybe she took a different route. In the next split second of my thoughts, I decided she was probably hurt and laying in a ditch somewhere. Well, that was how I usually think. I go from sane to absolutely insane thoughts, from the most plausible to the most far-fetched and improbable thoughts. I was parked in his driveway, so I sat in the truck, and tried to think about what to do next. I decided to go up to his house and ask him what he knew.

He answered the door and I could see that Lisa was there, standing behind him and she was looking rather sheepish. Of course he had to tell me she was there, because I could see her. My question to him now changed from "Is Lisa here" to "Where is Lisa's bicycle?" They were a couple of smart cookies all right. She had taken it into his garage. Now, I don't know if that was for safe keeping, so it would not get stolen or if it was to hide the evidence so I wouldn't see the bike if I drove by. Didn't matter. I found her, safe and sound.

Once again, I loaded a bicycle in the back of the truck, but this one was even more difficult. Having those two large tires in the back, plus the regular back tires of the bicycle, made lifting and maneuvering the bike onto the truck bed a little more challenging and awkward. But again, with their help we got the job done and Lisa was ready to get in the truck. Lisa knew I was upset with what she had done, taking off without asking, without writing me a note and without thinking about the consequences. She didn't even try to give her boyfriend a kiss, but got in the car and gave an embarrassed, pitiful wave instead.

When Lisa and I got home, she helped to unload the bicycle, and then went to her room for a while. Later, she came out and handed me a note. It said, "Mom, I am sorry. I shouldn't have taken off. I will tell you whom I'm with and the time I will be home. Or I will call. I got the hint. I should have known better. You can send me to bed without my dinner." That last sentence was odd because I have never nor would I ever send any of my children to bed without their dinner. I'm sure Lisa heard that phrase somewhere and thought it was a just punishment. I like the consequence to fit the crime, and part of her consequence in this case was that she had to come home with me when I found her at her boyfriend's house. I also decided that she wasn't allowed to ride her bike for a short while. I hoped that was a just outcome for her actions.

The two of them never tried to do that stunt again, but they did stay together for a while. Then, as sometimes happen in life, things changed for the two of them. Lisa went on to have several more boyfriends before finding that one, right guy for her.

Tattoos

Lisa was an adult, living on her own, working and making money. Then one day, she came up with a question for me. She wanted a tattoo. Since I knew nothing about getting a tattoo, I asked Lisa and a staff person to research the topic by going to a tattoo parlor and asking questions. When they gathered the needed information, I was told about the tattoo parlor, who would do the artwork, the cost and care of the tattoo and other questions that were necessary before proceeding with getting a tattoo. When I asked for this information, I thought it would take awhile for them to act on this request from me, so I thought I'd have time to think of reasons why Lisa couldn't have a tattoo. But, then I didn't think it was right for me to dictate my thoughts and point of view and say no, especially since Lisa was an adult and could decide for herself. And, I know what she would want to do; get a tattoo. They got the answers quickly, so I had a visit with Lisa and we came to an agreement. She could have a tattoo but I wanted to be a part of what kind of drawing it was, where it would be and how big it could be. The cost was also a consideration, because I told her I would not pay for it. She had the money, so that wasn't an issue.

The tattoo parlor artist came up with a nice design to put on her ankle. I didn't go to any pre-appointments or on the actual day the tattoo was done, because I didn't like the idea of someone etching on their skin to have a permanent piece of artwork on their body, especially when that person was my daughter. Lisa says it didn't hurt, but I can't believe that is possible. A needle drilling ink into your skin, over and over; that had to hurt. Lisa was given instructions on keeping the area clean and moist and when to change or take off the gauze covering. She was pleased with the results and for most of the spring, summer and fall she would wear low cut socks so her tattoo would be visible to her and others. And, she was always willing to show it off every chance she got.

A few years later, she wanted a second tattoo. I was not thrilled with this request but listened just the same to her reasonable rationalizations; where she wanted it on her body and that she did indeed have the money. Okay, so tattoo number two was decided on and a done deal fairly quickly. And, then there was a next time. Yes, a next time a few years later. I was really not thrilled at all about a third tattoo. Lisa and her staff person had always taken care of the appointment, the design and the care of the tattoo situation and I really did not have to do anything, yet I didn't like the idea at all. Somehow, Lisa managed to state her case, again, and she was going to get another one. As with each tattoo, all I asked was to have some input into the design, size and placement. Part of the placement of the tattoo was due to the rules of the establishment where she was working at the time. The restaurant did not allow any tattoo to be visible on their employees. Tattoos had to be hidden, by wearing something to cover up a tattoo on their arms, legs, neck or elsewhere. So, Lisa always chose places where it could be hidden with socks or shirts, but could also be shown off if she wanted to. And, of course she did.

There was one last tattoo and I really mean last tattoo. Lisa agreed to not having any more either. (I think I convinced her that they were getting too expensive, Lisa's comment, and that it really doesn't look so good when you have too many tattoos, my comment.) The fourth tattoo was on her upper arm and very nicely done. I actually went down to the tattoo parlor to visit with the artist and be a part of choosing the design instead of in past times where I would just be shown a sketch of what Lisa had wanted. A few days before the appointment to get the tattoo, Lisa called and asked to go shopping for some summer tops. Now, I knew that she already had plenty of summer tops but I figured she probably wanted something new to wear. Well, she did want something new, but she also wanted them to be tank tops or sleeveless shirts. It was so she could have easier access to the upper arm area, to keep the new tattoo clean and moist during the healing process. And, of course then she would also have more shirts to wear to show off the artwork. I don't know how or why she did it, but she now has four tattoos. They were good choices, nicely done in their design and colors. Hopefully, that will be the end of it. We'll see.

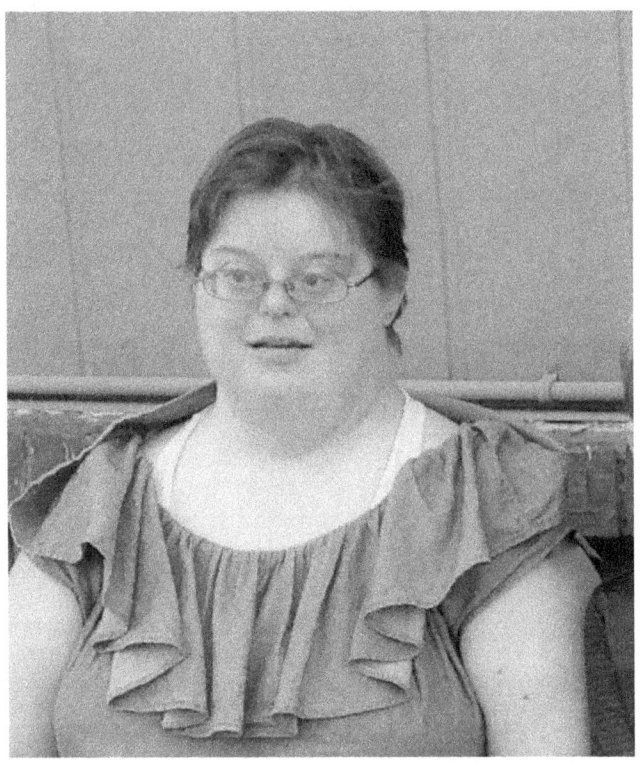

Ears Pierced Again

Lisa had wanted her ears pierced when she was in grade school and on the second visit to the store that did piercings, she finally fulfilled her wish; holes in her ears. She did well with the care of the ear lobes, cleaning them daily being the biggest and most important task. She had a small calendar that was given to her when she had her ears pierced and that was marked off with six weeks of boxes, showing the start date and end date for the structured cleaning schedule. Lisa used the bottle of solution that was given for this purpose and faithfully cleaned her ear lobes three times a day as directed. She even made three check marks in each day's box, showing that she had completed the task. She was very diligent and mindful of this responsibility, and the holes in her ear lobes never suffered the consequence of getting infected. She was also instructed to turn the posts of the earrings daily, which she did on a regular basis. After six weeks, life with pierced earrings was no longer a big deal, except when she went looking for more earrings to buy.

Lisa loved all kinds of earrings, but I usually tried to steer her away from any long, dangling styles. I also didn't think it was a good idea for her to wear any style other than the post earrings. The wire ones could be a hazard, as they could get ripped out of the lobe or any other such mishap that might occur with having something other than the post earrings. This was, of course, according to my personal knowledge of earrings and my lack of experience in wearing the long, dangling styles.

She changed her earrings occasionally, when she wanted something different to match what she was wearing or when she was going to be dressed up for something special. Lisa ended up getting a second set of holes in her ears when she was in high school, so she could have two holes in each lobe to accommodate the much anticipated new look of having two earrings in each ear lobe. Getting those second set of holes was no big deal for Lisa, since in her own words to the clerk who was ready to punch holes in her ears, "I'm a pro at this; I've done this before." I didn't give her ears or her earrings another thought, until one morning when she was getting ready for school. She got up, got dressed and came out of her bedroom to join us for breakfast. That's when I noticed her right ear lobe had some dried blood on it. My first thought was she had a ruptured eardrum and possible ear infection was to blame. That was not the case. Some how or other, during the night, Lisa's earring was torn away from her ear lobe. I thought that maybe I could help the ear lobe heal by squeezing the ragged, torn edges together and using a small bandage. I tried to keep it held tight together in the hopes that it would grow back together. That did not work. Duh! After several days and several different ways that I tried to keep the lobe together for the healing to begin, I was finally resolved to the fact that there would be no way for the edges to grow back together. So, Lisa had one lobe with two earrings while the other lobe had one earring and one ugly tear. It really didn't look too bad, but I felt bad that it had happened, even though I knew there was nothing I could do to prevent it or to fix it.

At some point after her high school days, Lisa decided she didn't want to wear earrings any more. I told her that would be okay because that I thought, if she ever wanted to wear earrings again, we would just clean the lobes and put her post earrings in again. Well, I was wrong. I had always assumed that once the lobes were healed after having holes punched in them and the posts stayed in place for a while, that the holes would always be there to use. But, the earring holes in her lobes grew shut. And of course, after many years of not wearing earrings, she once again wanted to have pierced ears.

So, we went to the nearest store that did ear piercings and went through the entire process again. Lisa was a little braver this time than she had been for her first and second times of having her ears pierced. In fact, before the lady was even ready, Lisa had climbed up into the chair. I say climbed, because it was a tall, highboy type of chair. I suppose that was to allow the ear piercing to be at a better level for the clerk. Lisa also talked about how she knew what was going to happen next, explaining it to the person who was patiently waiting with the ear gun in hand. In quick succession, both ears were re-pierced, in the same spots as the first piercings.

We went over the routine again about cleaning the ears, and being careful with the types of earrings that were better suited for her. I thought this would be the end of it, but no, Lisa wanted more earrings in her lobes. I think she noticed other people's lobes, and saw that the younger age group had at least four earrings on their ears. Since she had already had four holes, I thought it was possible, but the torn lobe was still an issue. We went back to the same store, talked to the clerk, and Lisa decided she would just have one more hole in one lobe and leave the torn lobe to have only one hole. It sounded good to me, and Lisa would now get a bargain when she buys other pairs of earrings. Because when she goes to buy two pairs of earrings, at least one of the earrings will be a back up, since she only has three holes. I'd say that was a bargain.

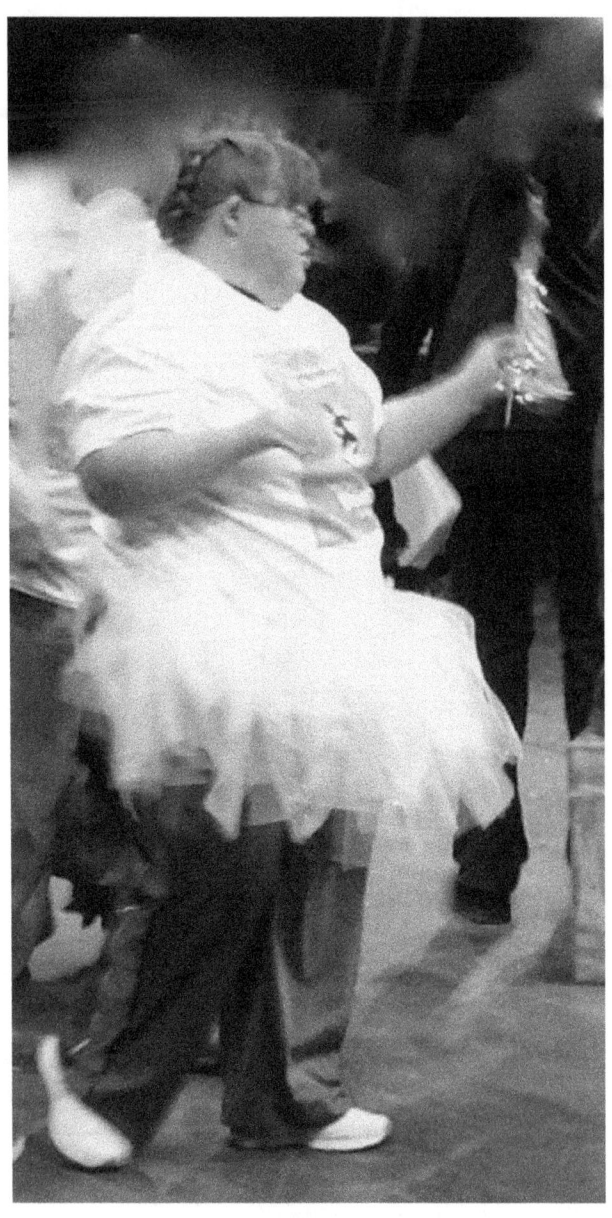

Plays And Talent Shows

Lisa has always loved being on stage with a microphone in her hand. When she was little, she loved to sing and dance. She had pretty good rhythm and a pleasant voice. Grade school performances were always fun to watch, even if the only things we saw were her smiling face and wiggly body. Lisa was also quiet and shy, never displaying the appearance of a person who might be made for the footlights on a stage. But, I have seen her grow out of her awkwardness and apprehension, and she now enjoys the spotlight whenever she can. A memorable time when Lisa captured the hearts and the laughter of many was at the wedding of one of her brothers. The venue was outdoors but the reception was under a large, pole tent awning that allowed for the best coverage in case of rain. This was where the meal was served and where the dance was to take place. In between the activities, there was a time for others to step up with congratulatory offerings and best wishes. There was the best man who spoke kindly and a few brave friends who had a few funny jokes to offer about the couple. Then I saw Lisa stand up, grab the mike and she began to talk to her brother and his new wife. She said some kind words about both of them, remarked that she loved them and finished with saying, "I'm watching you with my right eye and my other eye, too." That got a few chuckles and I realized that Lisa still liked to be in front of a crowd if she had a mike in her hand.

One of the places where Lisa works has a yearly talent show. Lisa usually joins in each year, singing with a choir that was formed at this workplace. She is never front-and-center with a mike, but she is singing with gusto and with a look of deep concentration as she is very serious about her singing and always wants to be sure she is doing the correct actions the singers had learned, as well as keeping up with the beat of the music. The choir always sounds great and the songs always peppy and uplifting. This same choir also sings at different establishments in the community on occasion, such as during the Christmas holiday season, going to nursing homes to bring a little joy and happiness to others. They also sing at a yearly awards ceremony for those who work where Lisa works. The staff, and the co-workers from Lisa's work place who are in the audience, all enjoy the choir's songs and cheerful attitude. If there's dancing, Lisa is right up front with her hip-hop moves and famous splits. Again, there is no mike when she's dancing but she seems to be on cloud nine just the same, dancing to the music.

Lisa also goes to an acting class weekly and twice a year they put on a play for the public. This class is offered through our town's local parks and recreation department and all those who participate are people who have a developmental or intellectual disability. Twenty to thirty people, who all want to join in the fun of learning a new story to tell or redoing a favorite movie, usually attend the weekly classes. A couple of the regulars who attend have also had a hand in writing some of the shows and these shows have been a real hit. Those who attend this class always have some input on what they might want to do and how to change parts of the program to suit their likes or capabilities. Whenever we attend these plays, we always enjoy how the cast has come together to make it work for them.

Lisa has been doing this activity for many, many years. Some of the shows she participated in were Peter Pan, Beauty and the Beast, Wizard of Oz, and many others. One show that the cast brainstormed and wrote as a group was a musical montage of country western music and dancing. I remember this one specifically because Lisa's dad and I were asked to attend a class session to help the cast learn how to do a square dance routine. This came about because Lisa shared with the group that her dad and I did square dancing. Well, we took lessons in country western dancing, but knew nothing about square dancing. Nevertheless, I went on a web site or two, learning all I could about this dance style. I set up a few easy steps, turns and routines that could be easily taught and learned in a short amount of time. Most of the time, square dances are called by a person who keeps the dancers in sync while taking steps to the beat of the music. So there wouldn't be a need for a caller, some of the easier steps I included when we went to teach the others the steps were Bow to your partner, Bow to your corner, Do Sa Do and Promenade.

Lisa's dad and I had fun teaching and dancing with this group of interested and willing participants. Because we had learned to dance the country western style, they asked us to demonstrate some of what we learned years ago. So we showed them a few of our basic routines that are easy to learn such as the Swing, Two-step and a little Polka. When the dance instructions were finished, Lisa's dad and I grabbed a partner from the acting class and started dancing. In turn, we told all the others in attendance to find a partner and dance. I had quite a few different partners in the ten minutes of spontaneous dance and I had a ball. These actors had been very attentive and quickly learned the steps that Lisa's dad and I had demonstrated. Going to watch that specific acting class production was extra special, because I felt a bond with all those who were polite enough to sit through our instructions of the square dancing and I saw how they put together what they learned to make a wonderful show.

This parks and recreation department has a form that is filled out yearly in order for Lisa to be able attend the classes they provide for people with developmental and intellectual disabilities. They also need a permission form signed for times when there is a trip offered, that includes individual medical information, and parent/guardian information in case of an emergency. These forms that we have to fill out are a simple request and easy to complete, especially for all the fun and experiences that Lisa has had throughout the years.

National Self-Advocate Convention

Lisa wanted to go to the National Self-Advocate conference that would be held in California. Cost was a factor, but we were able make it happen. Chaperones or volunteers were needed and many people helped to make it possible for Lisa to attend. Entertainment and activities would be part of a fun conference weekend. Let the excitement begin.

(The following account was written in collaboration with Hal's stepfather. Hal was Lisa's life partner for almost ten years.)

On this organized trip to Anaheim, California in a hotel bar-restaurant, a young man from a large city in Kansas met a young woman from a smaller city in Kansas. They were seated with two acquaintances who worked in the field of developmental disabilities and who introduced the two of them. The young man and young woman spent a lot of time together during the conference, repeatedly encouraged by the two who made the initial arrangement for the young couple to meet.

That young man, Hal, made connections with an organization in the city where the young lady, Lisa, lived. That non-profit organization hired him for a job. Hal would then tell his unsuspecting mother that he was moving because of the job, but he may not have told her it was also because of Lisa. After he moved away from the big city, Hal and Lisa met again at different local activities and thus began their time together. From this beginning, a respectable relationship began where they got together for sponsored social activities, to watch television, talk of their day's activities, go for walks while holding hands and visit her gracious family.

He was a young man with Cerebral Palsy and she was a young woman with Down syndrome, but that is of minor importance to the story. It was their caring for each other that invigorates this story. Happiness comes too seldom not to make an opportunity for two compatible and affectionate people to establish a commitment to each other. They decided they wanted to be together forever and thus began the idea of a commitment ceremony and celebratory reception.

Naturally, the ceremony would be where the young woman lived, but when? It happened on a Saturday in September with clear skies and temperate weather; a break from the stifling summer heat and the chilling winter cold. Where? A location that permitted a garden ceremony of commitment and indoor festivities of guests mingling, dancing, eating, and celebrating the couple's commitment without fear of a sudden rainfall.

First, there was a wedding shower, hosted by Lisa's older sister, who lived in another state. Invitations were sent out and those who could or would travel the distance did. What a fun and happy time, watching the two of them sitting side by side on the couch, holding hands and smiling constantly at each other with each gift they opened. Of course, the silly jeweled tiara of Lisa's and tall, black stovepipe hat of Hal's that they wore might have been part of the reason they were smiling so much.

Next was deciding where to have the commitment ceremony, and silly me, I thought it would work out great to have a small, private family gathering in our terraced backyard. I thought maybe thirty people or so, but I did not have a good grasp on who might want to attend, so I put out a query to family and friends about this issue. I also asked Lisa and Hal if they had any friends they would like to invite. Wow, was I surprised by their list. They had a *long* list. As the names kept coming in, through phone calls, emails and letters that were mailed, I realized that the small, quaint, family gathering in the backyard was not to be. When the invitations were finally sent out, there were between 75-100 people invited to share in this wonderful occasion. One of my favorite parts of the invitation was an Irish blessing embossed on the invitation which read, "May your hands forever be clasped in Friendship and your hearts forever be joined in Love."

After much thought, the perfect location to have the ceremony was found. It was the Union Pacific Train Depot. While the depot building was no longer used as a train depot, its days were extended by refurbishing the building as an event venue, including facilities for food service and meeting or dancing areas and the development of a beautiful entrance garden that complemented the renewal of the depot building. Thus started the first step towards Hal and Lisa's commitment ceremony and the rest of their lives, together.

Next, we had to think of the food and entertainment. The local grocery store chain was the most reasonable, so I went to check out their options. I had Lisa along with me, and we flipped through the wedding cake book, which had many, many options of cakes, flavors and decorations that would adorn the cake. Between the time Lisa and I made that first visit, until the next time when Hal was a part of the process and decision making, Lisa had used her artistic talents to draw several different versions of the cake she had envisioned. She had written 'Angel food cake' on one drawing that looked like a flat sheet cake and she had it decorated with a woman's tiara and a man's crown on the top. Another cake looked like it was a volcano with red lava oozing down the front and the top was marked 'pineapple.' A third drawing depicted a three-tiered cake identified as the 'Palm tree wedding cake' and Lisa had listed other items that seemed to be decorations on the three cakes, such as purple passion mints, pineapple and pipe cleaners. (Don't know what the pipe cleaners were for, except maybe they were a decoration of some sort.) For all three of these cake drawings, she had this list: color-brown and red; red pineapple, brown and white coconuts, a shape like a volcano, white mints and pineapple, yellow and turquoise blue pipe cleaners. Then she wrote, "Not in that order." The theme that Lisa and Hal had picked was Hawaiian; thus the reason for the pineapples. The cake ended up being delightful, with three tiers beautified with fondant frosting, a decorative three-heart ornamental piece and pink, yellow and orange buttercream flowers. Each tier was a different flavor: almond, spice and strawberry. And, on the side there was a marble sheet cake with the same frosting and flower design.

The next time we went in for a face-to-face discussion with the chef, he discussed the wedding cake and food options. Both Lisa and Hal had definite ideas about the food and Lisa had two pages of suggestions to share their thoughts on what foods they liked. We ended up doing a buffet style meal, with coconut tilapia, lemon pepper chicken breast, summer fresh pasta, au gratin potatoes, green bean casserole and key lime pie. While we were with the chef, we were able to have samples of the different cake and frosting choices as well as some of the buffet items and that was really fun.

We spent some time deciding on flowers, again choosing to use this same local grocery store chain, as they had very nice selections at a decent price. We purchased boutonnieres and corsages for honored guests such as parents, stepparents, grandparents and immediate family members. There was also the traditional bouquet of flowers for Lisa, and then for some reason there was a mention of flowers for Lisa's hair. She was going to have her long brown hair braided and she thought it would be nice if there were flowers in her hair. We ended up having a halo of flowers made, so it would be easy to wear and it would stick with the chosen Hawaiian theme. Lisa was thrilled with the results. As we were discussing the flower choices with family members, and more specifically with the young flower girl, it was decided to have the flower girl also wear a halo of flowers. But wait; there were two other nieces who were involved in the ceremony. It was decided that they would also wear a halo of flowers. The theme was starting to take hold, with lots of flowers involved.

The last, and according to Lisa, a very vital item to consider was a repertoire of music that would be used as entertainment and dancing after the banquet. Lisa wrote down many of her favorites for her brother-in-law to choose from, as he would be the designated disc jockey for the evening. Lisa had two pages of songs to add to the already chosen list of wedding songs and dance music that is common at a wedding reception such as the chicken dance, the hokey pokey and the electric slide. Oh yes, those were played over and over, but Lisa chose other songs too, like A Whole New World from Aladdin and Can You Feel The Love Tonight from Lion King. She had also written down a few others on her list, but then it looked like she crossed them out and added a note after those choices that said, "Don't pick this." She knew what she wanted and was very diplomatic and thorough in the decision-making.

With all the decisions made and as the date moved closer every day, I was constantly reviewing my notes and asking others for help to be sure I hadn't missed anything. I would occasionally think of my initial backyard plans and wondered how we got from that starting point to all the preparations of a much larger gathering. I felt that this was a once in a lifetime event and we should allow Lisa and Hal to have the type of commitment ceremony that they envisioned. And, I'm so glad we did it up right; it was wonderful.

Lisa, in a beautiful ankle length, white sleeveless dress, white veil, tresses properly styled and holding a bouquet of flowers, and Hal, in a suit and recent close haircut, were temporarily separated from each other, waiting for their special occasion to begin. What would the commitment ceremony be like, each of the two wondered. Hal's mother, Susan and I were on hand to lend emotional support to Lisa and Hal, as they were both nervous and yet eagerly waiting for their commitment ceremony to begin.

In the picturesque flowered garden on a sunny, fall day chairs were arranged for the guests; a wedding canopy stood under which the ceremony would take place and which represented their future home; and a sound system was installed to cover the expanse of the guests in the garden and to compete with the noise of the passing trains that traveled behind the train depot. The trains' whistles were usually short lived but loud, and once or twice the person using the microphone had to either wait for the trains to speed by or repeat what was said after the trains were further away from the station.

There was also a table to hold a prayer shawl that would be worn jointly over Lisa's and Hal's shoulders demonstrating togetherness; candle holders with lighted candles representing the enlightenment that Lisa and Hal would bring to each other; a loaf of twisted bread representing the stamina needed to work together to assure a life of peace and harmony; a cup of celebratory wine representing the commitment to live a joyous life together; and a thin wine glass in a cloth bag to be broken at the end of the ceremony to remind all that even at this happy time in the lives of Lisa and Hal, the world is still broken and needs the work of us all to bring about its repair.

Among the guests were Lisa's dad and I, Hal's mom and stepfather, as well as other family members and relatives from both sides. Others in attendance were friends and staff of Hal and Lisa's social and work community who gave on-going assistance and support to those who participated in that community. They had wide smiles knowing that two members of their community, Lisa and Hal, had found each other and were about to live a life of happiness together. As expected, there was much joy among those taking part in the commitment ceremony. *Lisa's immediate family members and Hal's immediate family members beamed with as much happiness as the participants.* It was mutually agreed that the ceremony be written and led by Hal's stepfather. I felt he had a way with words and strong values, and would be perfect to write and lead the ceremony. *He is not and was not a clergyman nor a lawyer nor any kind of official, but his strong familial feelings for both families made him an appropriate choice for writing the ceremony. The writing of the ceremony took into consideration that Lisa came from a Christian background and Hal came from a Jewish background, so common ground between the two traditions found its way into the ceremony.*

I remember when Hal's stepfather and I first talked about the ceremony, we discussed the religious background of both Lisa and Hal, and we decided that each of us would pick out three Bible verses. From that pool of six choices, Hal's stepfather would use three during the course of the service. Emails were sent back and forth, with different suggestions on how the entire ritual would be performed. In sharing our chosen Bible verses, we had each chosen two of the same passages. I thought that was an amazing achievement, considering the wealth of passages that could be appropriate for a ceremony of this kind. This was just one of many indications that this melding of two religions into one special service could be well done and very meaningful.

Lighted candles, ceremonial bread and consecrated wine are found in each of the two religious traditions. The meaning of the four cornerstones of commitment was read: love, companionship, devotion, and peace. God's blessings for loving commitments as well as the priestly blessing, among other religious values, were included within the ceremony. It might be said that this commitment between Lisa and Hal was founded in heaven.

Hal read his favorite Judy Chicago poem, "Merger," about how harmony in nature and harmony among humankind could bring peace to planet Earth. Hal dedicated that poem to Lisa's and his grandparents. The spiritual Apache prayer for commitment expressing the idea of two persons with but one life between them was also read. Additional readings and blessings were also delivered. Standing under the canopy, Lisa and Hal recited words of commitment to each other and exchanged rings, as they were led through the ceremony that included God's blessings for the couple.

Ending the ceremony in a traditional Jewish manner, Hal broke the glass under foot as the guests jointly said aloud "Mazel tov" which in Hal's tradition means "Good luck". Then, Lisa and Hal walked hand in hand to the depot building to begin the colorful celebration reception with a Hawaiian theme. Into the renovated depot meeting hall gathered Lisa and Hal, relatives and friends; some wearing leis around their necks in the Hawaiian style. A DJ played contemporary music, and one table held a tiered white wedding cake. Buffet tables, where catering personnel served appetizing cuisine and tables where drinks could be obtained, were also set up. Some guests sat in chairs lined up against one wall and many guests sat at tables and chairs on the other side of the room.

Lisa and Hal cut the first piece of cake, which they shared with much delight. They also were the first to dance, Hal, at a little over six feet, towering over Lisa at a little less than five feet tall. The difference in height did not betray their loving eyes gazing at each other. Soon many guests followed who danced to slow and fast music. All were having a good time as some drifted back to the buffet table to further partake of the refreshments. As the evening progressed, guests began drifting toward Lisa and Hal and family members to say their goodbyes. All left with smiles and happy thoughts of two people who found each other and who shared a mutual connection with love in their hearts. Lisa and Hal were soon whisked away to begin their new life together.

Two months later, on their first big trip without chaperones, they enjoyed their celebratory trip on a five-day Thanksgiving Baja cruise on the Carnival cruise ship "Paradise". Learning there were newlyweds on the ship, the ship's staff arranged a special wedding toast in the dining room for Lisa and Hal. What a fitting finale to the celebration of Lisa and Hal's commitment to each other.

And, now some ten years after this beautiful celebration of love, I remember a second blessing that was read during the ceremony and holds a special place in my heart. "May God bless and keep you. May God's face shine upon you and be gracious unto you. May God's countenance shine within you and bring you a life of health, of happiness and of peace."

Thank Goodness For Lisa

Hello dear readers! My mom, and the esteemed author of this book, has invited me to say a few words about Lisa to help tell a little of her story from a different perspective. My mom's first two published books featured artwork and stories from my brothers and my dad, and now you get to hear from me. My name is Tammy and I am Lisa's one and only "big sister."

As the oldest of the four kids in our family, I was technically everyone's big sister, but holding this official and all-important title became extra special when I finally met my little sister. Another girl in the house was exciting for me as a little girl with two younger brothers, and I was happy to take on extra big sister responsibilities when Lisa arrived. Growing up, I was her playmate, helper and certainly her favorite babysitter. Even when my parents hired some teenager to do the actual babysitting, I am sure I was telling the babysitter du jour how to do everything "just so" for my baby sister. Sure, I had had two brothers to watch over and admire but this was the sister that I had waited for, so it took on a whole new level of importance.

My seven-year-old self knew from the moment I saw her, that I would take this big sister job very seriously. I would do my best to watch over her and care for her and help her to become all that she could be. Lisa and I shared a bedroom for the first eleven years of her life, spending most every night sleeping in the same room and sharing the same space; with me listening to her snore and her listening to me talk in my sleep. There are seven years between us, so after I went to college, the lucky duck had the room all to herself. Well, at least temporarily, until I returned home again to invade her newfound space. School breaks, holidays and summer vacation found us sharing the bedroom once again; both of us happy to be temporarily reunited. Leaving for college when she was so young caused me to miss much of her growing up years, but we were still sisters and looked forward to time spent together, even if it meant I was occupying her room, as she did mine so many years ago.

I would like to think that Lisa learned a few things from me, and that I influenced the grown-up she became. I gave advice about hair, clothes, nails, friendships and how to antagonize your brothers; my particular specialty as the oldest of this crew. None of those seem particularly important for future life or career aspirations, but these activities were an important part of our sisterly bonding. Antagonizing of brothers aside, I tried to be a good role model for her. Providing big sisterly guidance was a job I took seriously and approached with love and care. As the oldest, and of course I thought the wisest, she needed me and all the wisdom I could impart, right? Right!

When I look back, I see that Lisa actually influenced me as much or more than I influenced her. Certainly, much more than I originally thought when I was dutifully filling my role of overly protective older sister, who would show her everything she needed to know and more. I had no idea at the time that she was actually guiding and influencing me, and the grown-up I would become.

And just who is that grown-up, you are wondering? I am someone who spends her days working in community building and philanthropy. I am passionate about helping to create a culture of giving, finding new ways to "do" philanthropy in business and nonprofits, and connecting people to the experience and joy of giving back. My husband and I own a small business in Nebraska, which is a billing and auditing service provider that exists to do good and be good. In addition to providing excellent service to our customers, our purpose is to make the world a better place through investments in our employees and in our community. In addition to my work with the business, I have spent the past several years working in philanthropy, charitable giving and community building with various nonprofits and community efforts. My work has been about giving back and encouraging others to do the same.

I am often asked how I "got into" this area of work, what makes me so passionate about it, and who most greatly influenced me. This is a hard question to answer, mainly because for a long time, I really didn't know. I did not set out to make "philanthropy" my career path. It is not what I studied for or imagined doing when I "grew up." But I believe this desire to serve has always been part of me and how I interact in the world, in large part because of Lisa and her influence on my family and me. Her entrance into our family is one of the reasons that I do the work that I do today.

Growing up, we were not a wealthy family by any means. My parents did not serve on boards, run for elected office or donate large sums of money to charities. I am not sure I even knew what the word "philanthropy" meant until I was an adult, and certainly I would not have considered our family to be "philanthropists" at the time. It is not that we were not generous when we could be; it's just that my parents were busy providing for and taking care of four young children. My parents are the sort of people who will help anyone who needs it, even during times when they had so little "extra." I know that they were involved in giving of their time, talent and treasure when they could, but it wasn't so obvious to me at the time. In the narrow definition of my young mind, philanthropists were rich people who gave away a lot of money, put their names on buildings and lived in fancy houses in neighborhoods other than mine.

All of that aside, my parents gave me many gifts that shaped my desire to give back. They taught me to care about others, showed me that family and community are important, that everyone can contribute in some way and that helping others is vital. I learned that life is full of challenges and everyone has them, no matter who you are, where you live or how much money you make. Much of life is figuring out how to navigate those challenges and make something good out of them; give something back to the world. My family learned about this in a very up close and personal way when my sister Lisa was born.

As you know, Lisa was born with Down Syndrome, which meant that she was different, at least as far as the official description goes. Lisa looks different than a person who has just the right chromosomes. She also developed differently than the rest of us. She was slower to accomplish physical development milestones such as rolling, over, sitting up and walking and it was harder for her to learn some things intellectually. But to three young siblings, all under the age of eight, she was just the newest and cutest addition to our family. One more seat at the table, someone to "help out with," and another person to get buckled in the van before we went anywhere. She was my baby sister and that was that.

  Looking back, I can see what a profound effect she had on my life and on all of our lives. She was really the beginning of my engagement in community work in a real way, because when Lisa was born, my parents began to more outwardly model the importance of service. They had a very personal reason to get involved. They volunteered to help people with disabilities, joined the Arc, started serving on boards and began to advocate for a more inclusive school environment and life for my sister and for all people with disabilities. And because we were young kids, the rest of us often tagged along.

  Not only were my parents inspired and mobilized by this unexpected change in their life, so were we. We went to advocacy and family support events, started spending time with more people who were different from us, learned what "disabilities" were, and what it meant to have a sister with Down Syndrome. We sold honey on Honey Sunday and participated in fundraising events such as the ever popular, and my personal favorite, Skate-a-thon. We began to see that even though we needed help learning how to help Lisa reach her fullest potential, we were also a family who could also help others. I experienced first-hand the desire to get involved and to help make things just a little bit better. I began my work in philanthropy as an eight-year-old girl who loved her baby sister and then grew to realize at that young age that sharing your gifts with the world is a powerful thing.

My work is rooted in the belief that "everyone can make a difference" and I know it has its beginnings in those early advocacy and fundraising experiences. Because of Lisa in my life, I am a more open and accepting person. Thank you, Lisa, for helping me to become who I am today, and thanks mom and dad for having the courage and the determination to get involved and show us what it really means to be a philanthropist. I am more willing to get involved in issues, projects and community efforts and I am very personally aware of what it means to have a reason to give back. I am, and always have been, grateful for my sister. She has added to all of our lives in such an impactful way, and I can't imagine life without her.

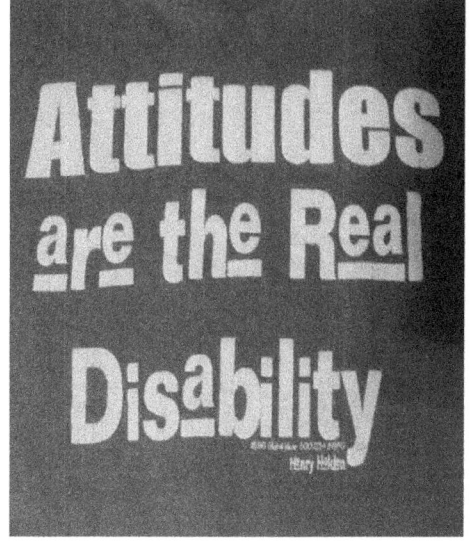

BARCUS

Anecdotes

1. When we made our last move from one state to another, we looked at the schools and what they had to offer before we looked for a house to buy. We began the house hunting process when we were satisfied with the school that Lisa would attend. We ended up in a nice, quiet residential area where the lawns were well kept, houses were neat, clean and affordable and where we found out how cordial and welcoming the neighbors were.

We moved in around July, just in time for Lisa to visit her new school once or twice before attending in the fall. We took a school tour, courtesy of a staff member and a teacher who would be with Lisa at certain times during the school year. Lisa was also able to become familiar with the bus schedule and school activities she anticipated joining. Lisa's dad and I both had full time jobs, so Lisa would usually be awake in time for me to know that she was dressed (appropriately) and had her breakfast before I had to leave for work. It was what she would do once I left for work that I found out later on through a neighbor. The neighbor said that Lisa would sit on the first step by our front door, talking to herself. Well, this was something I had already witnessed, even before I started back to work, so this wasn't too surprising. But, then the neighbor shared more. She told me that she would hear singing sometimes and look out her window to see Lisa in our driveway. The neighbor could see Lisa dancing and moving around while singing. I am guessing this was to keep herself occupied while waiting for the bus. I can also attest to knowing that Lisa is not shy when it comes to singing or dancing, so doing these performances in the driveway was really not a big issue, but I'm sure it was a delightful sight to see. The most interesting story this neighbor related to me was when Lisa walked across the street to the neighbor's house to visit at other times. It seemed to be around Thanksgiving or Christmas of the first year we moved to that neighborhood that Lisa made her first visit across the street.

    I know it was one of those holidays, because the neighbor remembers that many of her family members were there that weekend. As many as ten people were visiting and sitting around watching a movie on television and they invited Lisa to join them and to stay and watch, which she did. (I didn't even know she had crossed the street to go over there.) Now, I don't know if Lisa asked me if she could go over there or not because if I had known her plans, I may not have said yes because we really didn't know any of our neighbors real well yet at that point in time. If I had known her plans, I may not have said yes because I would have looked out the window to see that all those cars were parked around there, telling me that the neighbors were have company at that time. Either way, I don't think I knew where she went and that she ended up staying over there, visiting and watch a movie with them. The neighbor and her family talked to Lisa and found out that Lisa's birthday was about five to six months away. It would be her twenty-first birthday, which is a milestone for anyone. The neighbor lady asked Lisa what she was going to do on her birthday. Lisa's quick response, "Drink beer."

Lisa had not had much experience in drinking alcohol as far as I remember at that time. There was only one time that comes to mind and the story happened when she was probably fifteen or sixteen and we lived in a different town. There was one evening when Lisa's dad and I went out and both of her brothers were also gone for a couple of hours. Lisa was staying at the house by herself, which she had done a lot, so that was no big deal. When Lisa's dad and I returned home later that evening, I went to get some water from the refrigerator. I noticed a flavored wine cooler that was half empty. Someone drank part of it, then put the twist cap back on and put the bottle back in the fridge. The boys weren't home yet and I knew that Lisa's dad and I would not recap a wine cooler and put it back, we would have finished the entire bottle. My deduction was that it was Lisa and I didn't like knowing that. I never gave it a thought that she might try alcohol, any alcohol, without asking. In the morning, I asked Lisa what she had done the evening before while we were all out and her answer was that she watched television then went to bed. I asked Lisa how she felt before bedtime and she said fine. I gave up beating around the bush and asked her if she drank a wine cooler. At first, she just looked at me quite sheepishly. Then she said, "Not all of it!" I explained that it was alcohol and asked if she knew that, and she said yes. So I proceeded to explain that she wasn't old enough to drink, that it was against the law and she could be in trouble if she drank before she was twenty-one. She said she wouldn't do it again and I believe that was probably true. I had one thought that I wanted to share with Lisa, but didn't. My thought was, if she drank the entire wine cooler or drank half of it and poured the other half down the drain, and then just got rid of the bottle, I would have never known. I kept that thought to myself, because I didn't want to give her any ideas.

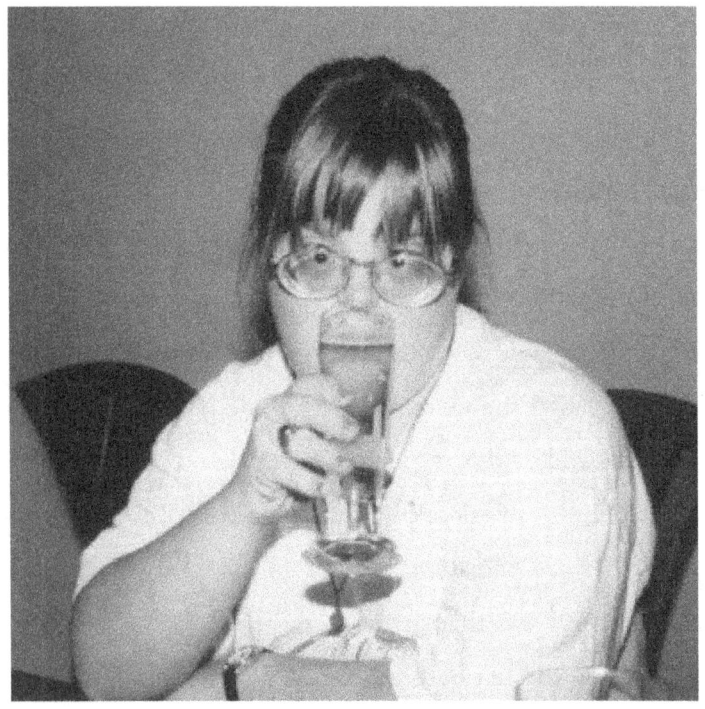

2. When Lisa sneezes, she doesn't just sneeze once, but multiple times. On a car trip one time, we counted a new high record, which amounted to at least seventeen sneezes in a row. Then, during one Christmas holiday season, Lisa was sitting in our living room and the Christmas tree was in the adjacent sunroom. Just as Lisa sneezed, she was surprised that the tree lights came on when she sneezed. She exclaimed she sneezed so hard that those lights just came on. The truth is, it was only by coincidence that she happened to sneeze at the exact moment when the timer was set to turn on the lights!

3. There are a few phrases that Lisa has said over the years that are a part of her thoughts and her honest frankness. Something she says quite often, especially when she has been looking for something that was really not lost, is "Oh, there it is." Just the way she says it makes you think the item was lost and that she had been looking for it for days. But the truth is she might have just said to me, "Mom, where is my …" and before she can name the item she was looking for she will say, "Oh, there it is." Lisa would also start to tell me something, trying to describe an event and she would hesitate mid-sentence, then look at me as if I would know what she wanted to say next. Then all of a sudden she would say, "What's that word?" Well, I didn't know where she was going with her story so I really couldn't figure out what word she wanted to say. We'd play this game of twenty questions, me asking what her story was about and if she could think of an easier word to tell me so I could figure out the word she wanted. Invariably it was a lost cause, because either Lisa couldn't come up with a different word or I couldn't come up with the topic of her story to try to figure out the word she wanted. It would be very frustrating for both of us.

A couple of other one-liners from Lisa include this short sentence that came up in the past when someone would tease her. She would relate the incident then finish with "It is not very nice to be mean." Also, when she calls me on the phone she will almost always say, "What'cha doing?" And if we are discussing a topic and she wants to give her thoughts on the subject, she will say, "Here's a theory."

4. Once, someone told Lisa that she was weird and her first retort would be "No, I'm not." Followed quickly by her quip, "Am I?" Another time, someone called her weird while we were in a dollar store. It happened shortly after we walked in and Lisa wanted to go to one section of the store while I was headed to buy some greeting cards. She was okay that we would do our own thing, so I told her where I was going then headed back towards the card section. It wasn't but a minute or two that I heard Lisa come around the corner, crying and almost running towards me. Of course, my mother instinct went into high gear and I reached out with open arms to envelop her in a big, strong hug. Once I calmed her down I asked what happened. She told me that a young boy called her weird. I tried to tell her that maybe he wasn't even talking to her but she was sure that he had directed that mean comment to her. So, then I told her that some kids don't know that is rude and maybe he didn't really mean it. I also raised my voice a little louder, hoping either the boy or the parent might hear me. I told Lisa that children learn what their parents and other family members say and that they should know better than to call someone weird. Lisa thought that made sense, and we finished up our shopping with her right beside me the rest of the time. Whether someone is perceived as different, weird, unusual, odd, peculiar or strange, that should not be how we describe people. We are all individuals with different traits and abilities. Let's hope we can all realize that. I have a quote from Winnie the Pooh that says, "The things that make me different are the things that make me."

5. Once when Lisa's right foot was sore and she was taking medicine to help alleviate the pain, I asked how her left foot felt by mistake. She answered, "My right foot is sore; my left foot is the good one."

Lisa doesn't usually wear hats, but there was one time when I picked her up to take her out shopping and she had a Nebraska ball cap on. I asked her if there was a football game that day and she said no, so I asked her why she was wearing a hat. She admitted she wanted to hide her hair, because it was greasy. I guess that's one way to handle the situation.

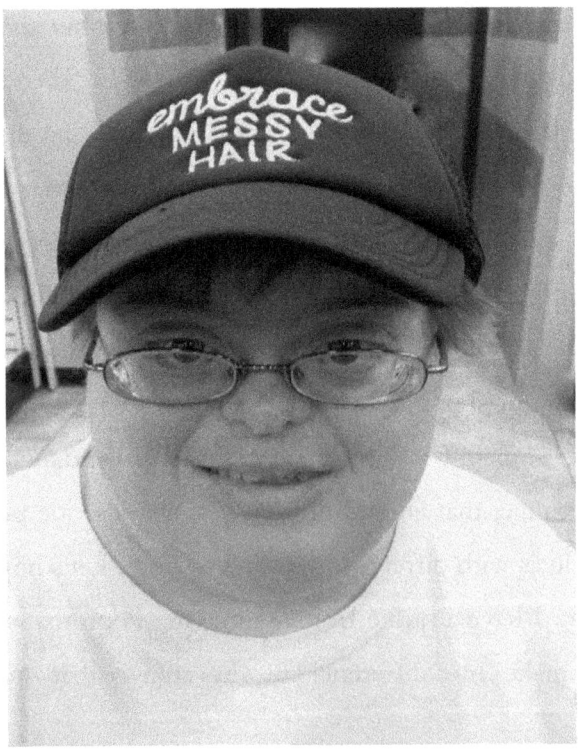

6. Lisa was on a big time lucky streak, with all of the following incidents happening within about a three week time period. I wish I had known it was going to happen all at once, because I would have taken her to go buy a lottery ticket. Her first stroke of luck came when Lisa was working at her job in the restaurant. She found a single $100 bill on the floor while she was cleaning up the front area near the register where the customers would normally stand to pay for their food. Lisa could have easily pocketed the money and had a nice little windfall. But Lisa, being the kind and honest person that she is, asked a nearby gentleman if it was his. He said yes, but did Lisa really know that for a fact? No, she didn't but she took his word as truth and gave it to him. As a reward, Lisa said he paid for her evening meal before he left the restaurant. They were both thrilled. The second time she had good luck, she found a single $100 bill when she took out her weekly garbage to the apartment complex dumpster near her building. She told me it was just lying on the ground and no one was around. She picked it up, went back to her apartment and then called me to ask what she should do about it. I told her that since no one was around, she could probably keep it. I thought about having her take it to the main office building but then anyone could say they had lost it and wanted to claim it. She did keep it and I thought "Good, now her budget will have a little extra money to spend for that month." That didn't happen. Lisa told me that she donated the money to her local self-advocate organization because they needed money to fund a project. She is always thinking of others.

The third time she found money was at her apartment. She found a few dollar bills in a pants pocket after washing her clothes one day. Then she said she found more money when she was going through some boxes that she had stored in her closet after she moved to her new one-bedroom apartment. That was another five dollars. She kept that for herself, enjoyed her recent good luck, and best of all, she enjoyed some extra cash.

Technology Talents

When I think of Lisa, one of her attributes is that she is able to figure out things that I wouldn't normally think she could solve on her own. Her mechanical abilities are few, but her determination and resolve are a plus. Once, she was given a pedometer to encourage more walking. You know, the whole 10,000 steps a day to good health. The problem was, Lisa doesn't like to walk much and never has. Case in point, when Lisa was a young grade school girl, she was clever enough to have a school classroom aide carry her when the class walked on an outing to the park. So, it's no surprise that as an adult with a pedometer to measure her steps, she probably never reached the 10,000 steps a day. Maybe in the entire time she used her pedometer, but never in a single day.

When we set up the pedometer for her stride, we showed her how to use the buttons and what they were for. She wore the pedometer faithfully for a while, and then slowly quit wearing it. But, during the time she wore it, she figured out how to check her steps, reset it as needed and work out any problems she thought there was if it wasn't registering her steps as she thought it should. Lisa also had a knack with the television and the remotes. She had one remote for the television and one for the DVR. At first, if she needed help, she would call us. If I went over to her apartment, I ended up being all thumbs and somewhat ignorant, not being familiar with her remotes and not being very mechanically inclined. Most of the times, Lisa would say to me, "Here, give it to me." and then she'd push a few buttons and things would once more be working properly. No thanks to me. At some point, if she called with a television or remote question and I answered the phone, Lisa would ask to talk to her dad. If he couldn't walk her through the problem, he would go over to her place to help. And, most of the time, by the time he got there, she would have the problem resolved. A few times, the issues would be batteries, so Lisa would try to replace the old batteries with new ones. The problem was that the batteries were usually in upside down and not all the way secured. I can totally understand that, since the plus and negative signs on the batteries are very tiny and difficult to see.

When Lisa got her first debit card, I wasn't sure she would be able to use it. I have trouble because the different stores have different machines, which are well, different. These machines ask different questions, have different buttons and different instructions when completing a transaction. But, Lisa only needed instructions once or twice, and then she got it. I would take her shopping and when it came time to check out, I would go ahead in line and just stand near the checkout counter in case she needed help. She usually didn't. Now, if I was going to purchase something when we were out shopping together, I would let her check out first, because that way I could watch what she did, what buttons she pushed and if a signature was required. It was just easier for me when I could watch her first.

She knew the routine. We did have to tell her that just because she has a card doesn't mean there is always money in her account. She has come close several times to being overdrawn. She now calls to see if she has enough money to buy something, so she doesn't have that problem any more.

When Lisa moved into her first apartment many years ago, she got a phone hooked up. She didn't have her own phone before this time, because she lived at home and shared the landline phone that we had in the house. Of course, she already knew how to use a phone, having proved that when she called 911 on two separate occasions when she was a young grade-schooler. This new phone for Lisa's apartment was a little different than what we had at our house but Lisa managed the variations easily. We set up her voice mail and she learned how to retrieve her messages. We also set up her contact list of numbers that she frequently used. But, Lisa rarely used this helpful function. She has an uncanny way of remembering her most dialed numbers, so she just punches in the correct numbers when calling someone. I couldn't do that now because I am dependent on the speed dial function or "last dialed" function. In fact, when I have to tell someone Lisa's phone number, I cannot remember it, but I can find it! Just give me a minute.

Lisa had an unlisted number because we didn't want everyone to have or be able to get her number for solicitation purposes. This worked well for a while, but somehow or another her unlisted number got out and she started to receive calls from businesses, the state patrol (who asked for money to support whatever project they were working on) and from other places trying to sell her things. Lisa didn't always know what to say to them to get them to stop calling. She was too nice and sometimes she even agreed to send money or buy something from these callers. After a few incidences where she was flustered and called us in a panic about the random calls, I think we got her to just tell the caller to not call again. And, later on she just didn't talk to them when they called. She would just hang up. (She always answered because I think it was just too difficult for her to let the phone ring and not answer it.)

Lisa has been through two or three sets of phones before getting a cell phone. We thought she could handle it, and hopefully not lose it. When a phone is mobile, not connected to the wall with a cord, it can be carried to every room in the house and it gets lost. Believe me, I know. I have had to ask Lisa's dad to call my phone on several occasions because I forgot where I last set it down.

At some point in time, we decided that she should switch to a different phone and phone service, because it was less expensive and hopefully a better solution for her to have this phone. There were times when we thought she should take her phone with her to work in the evenings, because she would sometimes get back to her apartment after dark. I worried that she could get locked out of her apartment, be stuck outside alone, without a phone, and not be able to reach us to ask if we could bring over the spare key to let her into her apartment. So, for me a cell phone meant security for Lisa. And, even though most of the time my negative thoughts never really come about, Lisa being locked out of her apartment did happen several times in the past year. I thought there was no way she could lock herself out of her own apartment, because if she ever left her keys at her apartment and went to work, the worse that could happen would be that the door wouldn't be locked during the time she would be gone. The positive aspect was it would not be locked when she returned, because the keys were left there to begin with. (There were a couple times when she got locked out of the apartment she shared with Hal, but that was usually because she forgot her keys, left before he did and he ended up locking the door when he left, not knowing that Lisa didn't have her keys.)

But, key and door issues have happened in her apartment a couple of times in the past. I remember I had walked Lisa through some explanations and reviewed the basics with Lisa when she moved into the apartment, like jiggle the handle, pull the door forward or push it inward and other helpful tips. I told her to picture the deadbolt going into jamb of the doorframe when she locked it, and it would disappear back into the door itself when she unlocked it. One evening, for whatever reason, her door didn't open, so she called us for help. I think what happened was that I totally confused her with my explanation, because she didn't have any problems with this door until after I tried to explain the mechanics of the deadbolt. She was finally able to unlock the door, and I was so thankful that she had her phone with her, because it was after work when this happened and it was also dark outside.

Another time when she called saying she couldn't get into her place, Lisa's dad went over with the spare key and returned home a few minutes later to share with me that Lisa had her keys but was not able to turn the key the correct way to get the bolt to unlock. Again, I think there was also a problem with the technique to get the correct position for the bolt to move back and forth smoothly. The second time she called that same week, Lisa's dad got on the phone and walked her through the process to get it unlocked. After that, there were no further problems, because I stopped trying to explain things to her. But, the good part of this story was that she was carrying her phone to work with her and she was able to call us to get help.

Sometimes Lisa might call me to tell me where she is going and ask if she needs to take her phone or not. Before I answer, my gauge is, will she be back before dark or at least before the main office of the apartment complex would close. My thought is, if the office was open she could walk over there to get their spare key to use. But, as far as I know, Lisa has not had to do that. And, I know she carries her phone with her most of the time now when she leaves her apartment, because she will call me when she is getting a ride to go to the store or to an activity. I tell her she could call me later, when she gets back home, but I think she likes calling when she is out and about.

The new cell phone was different than her landline phone. When she first got it we sat down to show her how to set up her voice mail, how she could easily find a name or number to call and how to use the emergency alert button. It is set up to notify my phone and it actually went off once. The instructions said that once set up, the emergency alert button needed to be pushed three times. Well, for some reason Lisa "accidently" pushed it three times and I was alerted. That was a scary moment, because I thought the worst not knowing that it was only by accident that it was pushed. Well, at least she knows what to do if she needed to, right? And, maybe she was just testing it out. I know I would want to make sure that the emergency alert button really worked. Just in case.

Her phone skills have improved immensely. There was a time when she first started using the cell phone that she would call and ask me if I had called her. She thought she heard it ring but couldn't answer it soon enough and the ringing stopped. I asked her to look at the name that showed up to see if it was a call from my phone. She said that she didn't see my name but still thought it might be me. So, I told her I would go over to her place and look at her phone and check it out. By the time I got to her place, which was just a few minutes drive, I tried to search her received calls and I could not find any. Her comment was that she deletes them right away. I didn't know she knew she could delete them. And, that's okay that she deleted them, but then I couldn't tell who had called. There was a time when I wanted to check to see who she was calling, because a couple of her phone bills were a little higher than normal. I asked Lisa if I could check her recent in-coming calls and she said that was fine. When I tried to search for calls received, again there weren't any. She had figured out that she could delete phone numbers from her call log and now she does that quite regularly. But because of learning that, I couldn't compare the billing with her recent received call log.

It was neat to find out that Lisa was interested enough in the phone's other features that she experimented with it to figure out what the phone could do. She discovered it could take pictures. And, she has a lot of photos of herself trying to take a "selfie." You can see her nostrils and maybe one eyeball, but not her entire face. This is because this phone does not have a reverse camera button so she has to turn the phone around, try to point it at her face without knowing what she was aiming at and then have a steady hand to push the button. I showed her the difference between my phone and hers, but she still keeps trying. The good thing is that now she knows how to delete pictures, too.

She says she has tried to text someone or send one of her photos to someone, but she doesn't have any Wi-Fi connections for that so the text or phone message can't be sent. I explained that to her and I don't believe she has tried to send photos or text since. But, the biggest surprise to me was that she found the games. Of course, all phones have games now, right? I figured something was up when I tried calling her one evening and she didn't answer. But, a few minutes later she called me to ask why I called her. I told her and then also remarked that I wondered why she didn't answer right away when I called. She said she was playing games. So I said something like, "Oh, you were in the back bedroom playing games on your computer?" She replied no, she was playing on her phone and wanted to finish the game before she answered the call. I was somewhat bewildered. I didn't know the phone had games on it. We have the same cell phone for our landline and I never knew about the games. And, suddenly I was aware of the fact that Lisa knew more about her phone than I did. But, then again she was always pretty good with figuring out things. She had a computer that was old but was useful for playing games. We loaded quite a few games on there and when I would visit she would show me certain games she liked to play. It looked like she had a pretty high score on some of those games, too. I didn't know she was that interested in playing computer games. I guess I still have a lot to learn about Lisa and the new things that interest her.

Lisa started taking her phone with her more often, so it was nice to be able to reach her during the day instead of waiting until she got back to her apartment before I would call her. With her landline, I would call her home phone any time of day, leave a message and hope that she would call me back. Calling her now usually means she will answer and I could get my question asked and answered right away. I try not to call during her work hours, but she has no qualms in calling me at any time during her workday. One time she even brought her phone to powerlifting practice and instead of keeping it in her coat pocket, she had it in her workout pants pocket. Before she was to go to the bar and do her practice lift, she would hand me her cell phone and ask if I would hold it for her. She said she didn't want to get a call when lifting. I guess she is getting use to having a phone with her at all times, just like most of us who can't be too far from our communication devices.

When Lisa calls me, we do this routine and the three and a half minute conversation does not vary much. The scenario goes like this: My phone rings, I pick it up and say, "Hello." Lisa is silent. Then I say, "Hi, Lisa. What are you doing?" Some times I might say, "How are you doing?" but either way I get the same answer from Lisa, "Not much." My next sentence is most likely going to be, "*What* are you doing?" Lisa's reply, "Not much." And, this is where we get stuck. I know she called for a reason, yet I want to wait for her to continue that conversation without my prodding. Most of the time I have to give in to the silence and say, "So, what did you call for?" With this comment she will say, "I have a question." And, from there we can get in to the nitty-gritty of why she called. She does a great job talking on the phone but sometimes she needs a nudge to get going. She has also called me unexpectedly, especially when her dad and I have been out of town for a few days. In that case, when I ask why she called, she would say, "I just wanted to check up on you." And that's the truth. Once in awhile when she calls me she might be feeling really good or have a great piece of important information to share with me, and I can usually tell because when I answer the phone and say "Hello," she pipes up immediately with "What'cha doing?" And me being the silly mom, I will answer the way she usually does with, "Not much."

Another more constructive and successful accomplishment Lisa has used her phone for was to solicit others by phone when she was trying to raise money for different fundraising events that she is involved in. She would call as many people as she could think of or that she had a phone number for, and from what I have heard she does a great job. Her sister, brothers, aunts and uncles have shared stories about how upbeat and positive she was in asking for a donation. Lisa would explain the nature of the call, what the fundraiser was, (which was usually a chili feed or pancake feed) who would benefit from the money that was raised and the time, place and possible suggested donation. She got the point across and usually received a lot of donations. Who knew that this quiet, reserved and soft-spoken person would be able to do so well with fundraising efforts? She is using a phone, so part of her success might be the fact that she doesn't have to look up at that person, which is something she has always had to work on through her years while in school. And, when talking on the phone about something that she believes in, she doesn't stop to let others comment but barrels right ahead with what is on her mind and what she wants to say. Her phone has helped her to open up, say what she feels is important and to be confident in her verbal approach. Isn't technology amazing!

Going To The Doctor

Going to the family practice doctor, eye doctor or dentist has always been interesting with Lisa. For example, taking her to her family practice doctor for a yearly physical exam got more detailed and somewhat more stressful as she got older. Just helping her to get on and off the scale when she was to be weighed was somewhat tricky. She needed to hold onto something to lift one foot on the scale and then hold on a little longer to lift and place the other foot on the scale. Her depth perception is a major issue, because it is difficult for her to look down and find where to step. She always seems a little unsteady when lifting one leg to step up onto something. Sometimes the nurse helped, sometimes I did. Once we were in the exam room, the nurse directed Lisa to the exam table. Just one look at that and Lisa knew she had to have help. So, I would be her stand-by assistant for help. She would put one foot on the step at the foot of the table, then she hung onto the side of the table to pull herself up to get the other foot onto the step that was about nine to twelve inches high. Now the dilemma for Lisa was how she would turn around. There is not much room to maneuver and nothing to hold onto, unless of course the table happens to be near the wall. I'd offer my hand and Lisa would very slowly and carefully inch her feet to turn herself around on that small area of the step she had to work with. The next issue had to do with Lisa's height. Lisa isn't tall enough to just sit down on the edge of the table once she is standing on the step platform, so I'd have to offer my other hand and arm to help her boost herself up onto the edge of the table. From there Lisa could inch herself up on the table's edge and scoot herself back to where she was safely sitting on the table. The entire process took a few minutes, which meant a little less time that we had to sit while waiting for the doctor to come in. And, there she would sit, with her short legs dangling because she couldn't reach the step to place her feet on for extra support.

    Lisa would occasionally ask me when the doctor would be in and I would look at my watch and give her a rough guesstimate, followed by my thoughts on why the doctor might be running late. Then, Lisa would ask if she could try out some of the toys that were in a basket next to my chair. Usually they were toys for little kids, but I thought, hey, if the toys keep Lisa entertained, distracted and relaxed until the doctor comes in, then why not let her play. Later on, I had a game on my phone that she liked to play, so that replaced the exam room toys. I thought that was more appropriate for Lisa and hopefully less germs on my phone than there might be on those toys that were probably handled by sick kids with a virus or something. No, I'm not a germophobe but I have some issues about knowingly sharing items with those who might have a virus or other such contagion.

    The next issue would be when the doctor came to do the exam. It's not too bad when she is looking at Lisa's eyes, ear, throat, neck or other areas of concern, but if the doctor asked Lisa to lay back on the table to palpate her tummy or check the swelling in her legs, then that was a new situation to be handled. The narrow table makes Lisa nervous for several reasons. She can't see where she is laying down and there is very little to hold on to in the process of laying back. The table is narrow, similar to a weight bench she uses when she does her weight lifting. In both cases, Lisa needs helped leaning back, finding her way to lie down in a supine position. In the case of being at the doctor, the third issue is the why she has to lie down, meaning there could be some unexpected surprises. Lisa doesn't like any surprises at the doctor's office so she needs to be told ahead of time about what and why things are being asked of her. Lying down on the exam table is definitely not what she wants to do, ever. She had been patiently sitting on the edge of the exam table, waiting for the doctor and now she is being told to lie down because the doctor has entered the exam room. I help Lisa again, offering her my hands and arms as extra support. I also offer a few words of encouragement, telling her to just lie back, that she has almost completed the task and I give her encouragement when she has managed the supine position. Lisa does best when she has something to hold on to while she slowly inches her arched back down flat to the table and over the years it has become easier and quicker. There is usually a need for Lisa to use her feet to push her self up to where the pillow is and finally I can let go when she is situated safely. But, she doesn't always seem to be comfortable and she is always holding on to the edges of the table so she doesn't roll or fall off the side.

When she's at the dentist office things are a little easier, though she is just as nervous as when she is at the medical doctor's office. Before we ever get to the dentist office, she is asking why we are going, even though I've already told her why. If it's a cleaning, she is okay with that. If it's dental work, I usually explain what they will probably do, whether she will need a shot to numb the area to be worked on or if they are doing x-rays. She has had fillings and crowns done, so she knows the ropes, but the worst part of her fear has to do with having fillings or crowns. I guess anything that requires being numbed is a clue to Lisa that she won't like the procedure. But, then she could have acquired that fear from me. I don't like fillings and crown work either. She has also had a custom-fitted mouth guard made for her, to prevent tooth damage because she grinds her teeth at night when she is sleeping. I guess she was very good about following directions, trying to open her mouth when the dental assistant was working on finding the correct mold size to use for Lisa's small mouth. Lisa also had to be patient when they were getting the impression of her teeth to be used as the mold for her mouth guard. A powdery substance is mixed with water and it ends up as a goopy mixture. It reminded me of play-doh. Then this substance is placed in an impressions tray and the person getting a mold done of their teeth, in this case, Lisa, had to squish her teeth in this mixture and hold very still while the substance hardens. Lisa's only comment with this procedure was, "It was icky and easy."

Lisa's favorite part of the visit has always been when the dentist or hygienist is finished with the work. She gets to pick out something from the kids treasure chest of small toys and items to take home. I get a kick out of this, especially since she has made it a habit to bring her backpack along to the visit. I wasn't sure if she brought it because she thought she might get more than one toy or she brought it because of what she might have brought into the dentist office, like her night mouth guard that gets cleaned during the visit. Of course, besides getting a toy she also receives a sample of toothpaste and a new brush, so maybe she thought that might be too much to carry without having her backpack. Which makes me think of another time when she brought her backpack somewhere and I wondered why. Lisa, her dad and I attended a Special Olympics fundraiser bingo night and when we picked up Lisa, she had a backpack. I wanted to ask her why she wanted to bring it along but I didn't. Well, it was evident when she won at bingo. She brought the backpack to carry all her prizes. She was so confident that she was going to win that she knew she would need it for that very reason. Usually the dental hygienist put all the free goodies and toy in a small, plastic bag that was just the right size. And yet, I would never tell Lisa not to bring her backpack, even though she didn't really need it. That was her thing and I am glad that she has enough foresight and confidence to always be ready. She was always thinking ahead with anticipation and hope.

    When Lisa would have her yearly eye exam, she was usually pretty good at following directions while in the exam room. I always try to pay attention to the assistant who takes her to the exam room and who is normally the first person to do a pre-assessment exam and who calculates the current script in the lenses. The assistant does some preliminary exams, using two different machines that check different things. One machine is an auto-refractor while the other one is an eye-puff test, or otherwise known as a non-contact tonometer (NCT). With the first test, Lisa has to just stare straight ahead while the assistant measures the shape and size of the cornea and get a base prescription. Lisa has to look in the machine at a red farmhouse and try not to let her eyes waiver. Lisa has trouble staring straight ahead but the assistants she has had in the past have always been patient with her, encouraging her in a positive way, saying things like "We are almost done," "Let's do this once more," or "You are doing great!" With the machine that calculates the intraocular pressure, which could indicate possible glaucoma, the staff person is still positive and encouraging, but Lisa would have nothing to do with that machine. Lisa knows from past experience that once she puts her chin on the chin rest and her forehead stabilized by a curved, cushioned headrest, there would be a puff in her eye and she doesn't like that. At her latest visit she became nervous when they directed her to the room where these machines were. Lisa walked sideways past the machine when she entered the small room, to avoid the nasty machines and she wouldn't sit down in the chair when asked to do so. Lisa's comment was, "Are you going to shoot cotton balls at my eyes?" Well, technology has come a long way because the assistant reassured Lisa that the machine no longer does a puff. So Lisa was able to get through both tests with little concern or dramatics.

  Lisa began wearing glasses at a very young age, so she doesn't know anything different. With glasses, she can see fairly well but without them, her vision is very compromised. When Lisa was a young adult, we had an opportunity to take a trip to the Cayman Islands, where we stayed at a condo and our backyard was a beach and the ocean. The coral reefs were beautiful, so we all rented snorkel equipment to experience them close up. I wasn't sure that Lisa would be able to snorkel, first because she didn't like putting her face in the water and second, because she wouldn't be able to see much of anything. But, we encouraged her to try and she actually did rather well. I would swim next to her and sometimes place my hand on her arm or let her put her hand on mine. We practiced keeping her face in the water, breathing through the mouthpiece, and using the snorkel gear correctly. She got the hang of all that fairly quickly. Then we started swimming around, looking for fish, sponges and seaweed that cover the surface of the reefs. We saw many beautiful, brightly colored reefs of blue, orange, pink, yellow and green. Lisa started swimming away from me toward other marine life and sometimes pointed out a colorful fish every once in awhile. Some of those fish seemed almost fluorescent in their coloring so they were easy to see; others were so small and less colorful, but Lisa saw them as well. Maybe the goggles helped with her sight. As it was, she could see the marine life and we had to urge Lisa to stop when the rest of us were done with snorkeling for the day. So, I am never sure how much Lisa can see but watching her snorkel let me know that she could see more than I realized.

Back at the eye doctor appointment, Lisa's eye doctor has had some problems, especially when he needed to dilate her eyes. Thank goodness this didn't happen every year. Lisa is better at reading the eye chart now but needs time to respond with the request to read each line. I'm usually sitting quietly in the room and I can see the different letters she has to read. Lisa used to hesitate on certain letters that are difficult to decipher, such as the letter O versus a G, or a T versus an I. Lisa would look at me and say questioningly, "Mom?" Like I was going to give her the answer. As she has gotten older, she now knows the routine and just powers through the letters as best she can.

There were several visits during one specific year when we had to take her to the eye doctor because of dry, red eyes that got gunky and crusty at times. Being a school nurse from years ago made me jump to the diagnosis of pink eye, but thankfully that was not the case. Initially, I was told to give her eye drops that would help to add moisture to her eyes and help clean up the gunk and redness. It was suspected that because Lisa has Sjogren's syndrome, her eyes would be drier than in the past. (This is one of the many signs and symptoms of Sjogren's, which is a chronic autoimmune inflammatory disease in which moisture-producing glands are damaged. It may affect many parts of the body, including major organs, but hallmark symptoms are dry eyes and dry mouth.) I was hopeful that the eye drops would help resolve this situation. I even went over to Lisa's apartment twice a day, several times a week and for several weeks to administer the eye drops, but to no avail. The symptoms persisted.

The culprits, according to the eye doctor, were her eyelashes. Especially the lower lid lashes. (Say that three times real fast!) The lashes were turning or curling into her eyes, thus causing the signs and symptoms she was exhibiting during those past few weeks. I guess this eyelash situation is common and actually has a name, which I can't pronounce. It is called trichiasis. It just means that the eyelashes have turned inward and they rub your eyeballs, which then causes the symptoms and problems that Lisa was having. Treatment was to physically pluck them out. Now this didn't sound good to me; it sounded painful. This eye doctor gave Lisa a choice of having it done at that visit or rescheduling to a later date. Lisa and I talked about it, with the eye doctor weighing in with detailed information as well. My thought was if Lisa didn't do it right then and there, she would not be easily swayed to have a return visit. When it was discussed enough to make a decision, Lisa said to go ahead and pluck away. The tweezers came out and the process was done.

Lisa was pretty brave, sitting there as still as possible while the eye doctor removed a bunch of the lashes from each lower lid. He finished by saying that they would grow back and the procedure might have to be repeated later on. That was not what Lisa wanted to hear. As it turned out, the eyelashes did grow back and if they are curled inward a little, it hasn't been a problem like it used to be. And, the best thing for both her and I is that she doesn't need the eye drops any more. But even though this problem has been resolved, Lisa always has some questions when there is an eye appointment scheduled. The first question is, "Is the eye doctor going to pull out more lashes?" and the second question is, "Is that lady going to puff my eyes?" To both I reply that I don't think so, but that we would find out when we got to the office. I think she just wants to be ready. So do I.

BARCUS

Sjogren's Syndrome

I was in Nebraska visiting family and one evening while reading the daily newspaper, I glanced at a column that was in question/answer form, written daily by a physician. I wasn't even thinking of Lisa at the time, but always enjoyed the medical information I could glean from the column. What hit me was a question on Sjogren's syndrome. As I was reading, I realized that Lisa could have that disorder. So, I researched the topic more on the Internet, and was then one hundred percent convinced that Lisa had that, too.

Per the Mayo Clinic website, "Sjogren's (SHOW-grins) syndrome is a disorder of your immune system identified by its two most common symptoms-dry eyes and a dry mouth. Sjogren's syndrome often accompanies other immune system disorders, such as rheumatoid arthritis and lupus. In Sjogren's syndrome, the mucous membranes and moisture-secreting glands of your eyes and mouth are usually affected first-resulting in decreased production of tears and saliva. Although you can develop Sjogren's syndrome at any age, most people are older than 40 at the time of diagnosis. The condition is much more common in women. Treatment focuses on relieving symptoms." [5]

The two main symptoms are dry eyes and dry mouth. The dry eyes might feel like there is sand in them or they might burn or itch. The dry mouth may cause the person to mumble or feel like there is cotton in their mouth and it may be difficult to speak clearly. Lisa had been more difficult to understand, but I didn't give it much thought at the time. And before Lisa was diagnosed, Lisa's eyes were itchy and red, so I had taken her to her eye doctor. He thought it might be her eyelashes that were turning in, on to her eyeballs and that caused the irritation. He took some type of tweezers and actually pulled many of those eyelashes out. He also recommended checking into the Sjogren's suspected diagnosis. Two ways to go were to have a test call Schirmer's test or by doing a biopsy of the glands in the lower lip. With the Schirmer's test, they use tear test strips. A test strip is placed under the eyelid for at least five minutes, from what I can remember the eye doctor telling us, and the results would show if the eye has the ability to wet this small test paper strip. There is also a more sophisticated test that can be done by an ophthalmologist. With the lip biopsy, a surgeon or an ENT (Ears, Nose and Throat) specialist would do a biopsy. The biopsy is done under local anesthesia and a small cut on the inner part of the lower lip is made so they can remove a small sample of the salivary glands.

While we were discussing what would be the easiest for Lisa, I remembered Lisa having a small lesion removed from her upper lip when she was about five years old. I was working for an oral surgeon, who said he would remove that and there would be little to no scar. I remember he used a local anesthetic plus a small amount of sedative to relax Lisa. Well, the surgery went well and Lisa tolerated the procedure. The only problem was afterwards. Lisa slept for quite a long time, and I remember that I did not want to lie her down in her bed because I didn't want her to rub her upper lip and take that chance that her stitches might come out. So, Lisa and I rocked a lot those first couple of hours, until she was fully awake and able to swallow comfortably. Her upper lip was swollen for a while, but when the stitches were removed she was in great shape.

Because of this prior surgical incident, I felt she would better tolerate that type of testing again, rather than having paper stuck to her eyelid. Or maybe it was just me; I didn't think I would want anything like that in my eye, even though I had worn contacts for many years. I wasn't sure how I could convince Lisa to allow that to happen, having paper adhered to her eyeball, because I knew from past experience that she didn't even like eye drops in her eyes. That was a challenge when she needed them and a lot of persuading and convincing. Bottom line, or should I say bottom lip, the biopsy won.

The doctor who did the biopsy was an otolaryngologist, which is an ear, nose and throat doctor. The procedure went smoothly for Lisa. She had a couple of stitches inside her mouth, on the lower lip. I am thinking that the stitches had to be removed in a certain time line, and then we found out that the test proved us right. Lisa had Sjogren's syndrome. There are other symptoms that might occur, such as dry skin, fatigue and joint pain, to name a few. I name these, because those were some of the other symptoms Lisa had been complaining about.

Sjogren's syndrome is an autoimmune disorder. That means your immune system attacks your body by mistake. It is not known why certain people get Sjogren's syndrome. It is suspected that something like getting an infection from a certain virus or bacteria can cause it. Besides attacking the glands of your mouth and eyes, Sjogren's syndrome can also do damage to your joints, thyroid, kidneys and skin, to name a few. I mention those, because she has medical issues with all those areas. From medicinenet.com, "When the tear gland (lacrimal gland) is inflamed from Sjogren's, the resulting eye dryness can progressively lead to eye irritation, decreased tear production, a 'gritty' sensation, eye infection, and serious abrasion of the dome of the eye (cornea). Dry eyes can lead to infections of the eyes and inflammation of the eyelids (blepharitis). The condition of having dry eyes is medically referred to as xerophthalmia. When the eyes become inflamed from dryness, it is referred to as keratoconjunctivitis sicca.

Inflammation of the salivary glands can lead to mouth dryness, swallowing difficulties, dental decay, cavities, gum disease, mouth sores and swelling, hoarseness or impaired voice, abnormality of taste or loss of taste, dry cough, and stones and/or infection of the parotid gland inside of the cheeks. Dry lips often accompany the mouth dryness. Dry mouth is medically referred to as xerostomia." [6] There are other serious considerations when it comes to having Sjogren's, but I have just focused on some of those issues that we know for sure Lisa has had to deal with.

From the information I have found, there is no cure for Sjogren's syndrome. The best we can do for Lisa is be attentive to her physical complaints and treat the symptoms. That would include artificial tears or eye drops for her eyes, having her use lip balm for her dry lips, drinking plenty of fluids, using a humidifier in her apartment and having good dental care to avoid any tooth decay and gum problems.

Once Lisa was diagnosed, it was recommended that she see a rheumatologist. She started off with one such doctor, and he prescribed medicine for her dry mouth. He also wanted to see her every few months, and I was beginning to wonder why, because nothing ever changed with Lisa's Sjogren's issues. When this doctor retired, Lisa started seeing her family practice doctor for her Sjogren's when she needed to, and that doctor prescribed the necessary medicine for Lisa. When Lisa had specific issues that warranted a rheumatologist, we found a new specialist for her to see. For a while, that rheumatologist just saw Lisa once a year, and for Lisa that seemed to be adequate because her symptoms were not serious enough to warrant a doctor appointment with the rheumatologist any more often than that. Lisa had felt bad when the initial diagnosis came back as positive for Sjogren's. I asked her why she was upset and she said, "Because now I have two syndromes." I felt bad also, and had no comment or funny comeback for her. She has dealt with this diagnosis and it's issues for many years, and it just proves to me that she can handle the situations with a sense of calm and stoic demeanor, and accepting what she has without complaints. She is a trouper.

BARCUS

Thyroid

Years ago, Lisa was diagnosed with hypothyroidism, which means that the hormone, thyroxin, in her body was decreased. Thyroxin promotes growth of the brain and other body tissue. In children with Down syndrome, according to the National Down Syndrome Society, it is estimated that approximately 10% of these children have congenital or acquired thyroid disease. It took me quite a few years to understand the blood work results and how the TSH (Thyroid Stimulating Hormone) controls the thyroid function. And if the TSH is high, then the drawn blood will also be checked for T4 levels. There's also a T3 level, but don't ask me about that! It's too confusing to explain; especially if I have to explain it, since I am still a little confused after all these years. So, I trust the lab techs to do the work and I trust the doctor to tell us what Lisa needs to do if the levels are too high or to low. A thyroid disorder can cause a wide range of symptoms. For example, you might have mental issues such as anxiety or mental sluggishness as well as physical problems such as fatigue, constipation, weight fluctuations, irritability and menstrual irregularity. Lisa has had all these symptoms at one time or another.

Between the time when she had her tonsils and adenoids out and when she started using a CPAP, Lisa started to gain a little weight. This was when I began to have an inkling that something was wrong. Her weight gain was slow enough that it wasn't an earth-shattering amount at first, but I soon realized that her clothes became a little tighter on her. I reviewed our laundry routines thinking maybe we had used hot water recently that shrunk some of her things. Then, Lisa started to complain of being tired and I noticed she was less active physically. Riding in a car even got to be an issue because she would complain of being uncomfortable in the back seat. When she tried to get out of the car, it was an effort for her to move her legs to step out of the car. Then to stand up and walk was even more difficult for her. She wasn't that heavy that she couldn't carry her weight but she was always really tired. I thought of many reasons why she could be having these physical problems. Was it arthritis or something else joint related? From what I have read, there are similar symptoms between rheumatoid arthritis and thyroid disorders. Overlapping symptoms include swelling around the feet and legs, muscle discomfort and weight gain. So, I guess I wasn't too far off in my thinking that it could be arthritis.

A few years after seeing the article on Sjogren's syndrome, I was again reading the newspaper in Nebraska that still had the physician's column on health issues that I always liked to read. What caught my eye was a heading that read something like "Joint issues related to thyroid issues." As I was reading, I kept track of all the symptoms listed, checking them off in my head as I read. Joint pain, check. Tired, check. Weight gain, check. There were more symptoms listed, but those jumped out at me because those were Lisa's complaints. So, my "professional" diagnosis agreed with this columnist doctor's answer. Lisa had thyroid problems. I then wondered, "What can I do about it?" The article recommended a lab test and talked about TSH, which stands for thyroid-stimulating hormone. This is produced by the pituitary gland, which is located below the brain and behind the sinus cavities.

I felt a little silly, calling the family doctor to ask if Lisa could have this specific lab work done, but her doctor was really good about it and ordered the labs. (Maybe because I was a nurse in my past life, she agreed to check it out or maybe it was because I felt so positive about the information and Lisa's signs and symptoms that the doctor was curious.) No matter how or why, the doctor ordered the TSH lab and the results proved what I suspected. Lisa had hypothyroidism. The diagnosis of hypothyroidism was now official because of the lab work with the doctor reviewing the results, and the beginning of when Lisa started to take any prescription drugs.

Hypothyroidism is a common endocrine problem in children and adults with Down syndrome. While I was researching Lisa's complaints and searching for answers, I learned that newborns with Down syndrome should be tested at birth and about every two years after that initial test for possible hypothyroidism. For newborns it is especially important, because the thyroid hormone can disrupt the natural development of the brain. Hum, I didn't know that when Lisa was born. Probably a lucky thing for Lisa because I would have faithfully had her tested every two years.

When she was diagnosed as an adult, Lisa started on a low dose of a medication and had occasional lab checks to be sure her levels were in the normal range, which would mean that she was taking the correct dose as prescribed. She did well taking this small pill and over time the labs were pretty stable. When there was a dosage change, I would explain the new prescribed amount to Lisa and the times she was to take the medicine. It was always a little different, sometimes one-half of a pill was added or a higher dose prescribed. Lisa adjusted to taking the medicines, even with the various changes that had to be made. Only once or twice did she have difficulties with the changes. One time it was because she went from one pill to a half pill, but I didn't take the time to break the scored pill in half for Lisa and she didn't think to do it either. When the next labs were done and the levels were not within the normal range, I knew something wasn't right. After that, I tried to check Lisa's medicine containers occasionally to be sure she had the correct pills in the correct containers with the correct amounts.

About six months after she was diagnosed with her thyroid deficiency, I noticed that Lisa was acting more tired again, wanting to go back to her apartment because she complained about being exhausted and seemed to me that she looked a little pale. I am always watching for any unusual changes in her looks, weight or habits and these complaints were of a concern to me. I thought that she might have a B12 deficiency. And now, I will tell you why I would jump to this conclusion. This is one medical health issue that I know quite a bit about. Years ago, I had similar complaints in addition to having some numbness and tingling in my right arm. After my doctor ran an electrical test called a nerve conduction velocity test (NCV), he wasn't sure what to do because that test came back negative for any nerve injury or abnormality. I mentioned that my grandfather died from pernicious anemia, which is an autoimmune problem and is associated with B12 deficiency anemia. My blood work came back showing my B12 was in the very low range. I started on an oral B12 medication and other than a few highs and lows in the lab work on occasion, I have been able to maintain my B12 levels with oral medication.

Having said all that, and knowing that I knew what I was talking about in the area of B12 deficiencies, I asked the doctor to run a B12 lab check on Lisa. I am so glad we did that. We eliminated any other tests that the doctor might have done and received the lab results that Lisa's B12 level was indeed low. Doctors are sometimes hesitant to recommend the oral B12 because part of the pernicious anemia difficulties occur due to stomach absorption, but since I had good success with the oral medication, the doctor decided to start Lisa with that, reserving the call to do injections if necessary. So far, Lisa has been able to keep her levels in a pretty good range.

Now, the thyroid, B12 and Sjogren's are some of Lisa's medical problems and they are all related to autoimmune problems. This means that the immune system can't tell the difference between healthy body tissue and toxin or foreign substance in the body. Lisa also has glucose levels hovering around the high end of the lab reference range that could develop into diabetes type 1. According to several different websites and medical journals, written in words and charts that I don't quite understand, people with Down syndrome have a higher incidence of autoimmune diseases. I remember being told when Lisa was about a year old that because she had Down syndrome (trisomy 21) she also had a higher risk factor of getting leukemia. According to the American Cancer Society site, there is a connection with some inherited disorders increasing the chance of developing leukemia and Down syndrome (trisomy 21) is one such disorder. Well, that news didn't make my day, but I decided to focus on Lisa and what we could do to keep her as healthy as possible.

One way was to always be diligent in Lisa's medical needs, which included making sure she took the correct medicines for the variety of medical conditions she had. Her plethora of medicines has always concerned me and I needed to always be on top of any issues when dealing with, organizing and helping Lisa with her medications. As an adult, Lisa has always been great at calling me to tell me when she was running low on a certain medicine. Occasionally, she would call me to say she was out of her medicine and then I'd panic because I knew if she didn't take her medicines on a regular basis as was ordered by the doctor, the next time labs were drawn, her blood levels would be out of whack. Then we would have to go back to the drawing board to either increase or decrease the dose until the levels were once again in the normal range. That's always somewhat frustrating, because it meant there would be few more visits to the lab to recheck her levels. She has been great with taking the medicine, getting labs drawn and being responsible to tell me when she needs more. I make it a point to occasionally go over to her house when she is filling her weekly medicine containers and just watch her while she is doing that. I might ask her questions like, "What is the name of that pill?" "What is that medicine for?" and "When do you take that white one?" She knows her stuff without reading the labels. And, that's a big accomplishment, because currently Lisa is taking quite a few medications. I have written up a sheet that listed all her medicines, when she takes them and why, and when they were first prescribed. I have a second section that lists what time of day she takes what pills and what case they are in. This should help when others might have to step in to assist Lisa with her medications. She uses four different medication cases to keep track of all her medications. Her morning medicines might be in the large clear case, her noon medicines in a round, blue case and her evening and bedtime medicines are in other easily identifiable cases. It is very confusing to look at each label to be sure she is taking the right medicine at the correct time if you are unfamiliar with the variety of medications she takes.

 Recently, I was making up new sheets for her since she had a couple of changes. (The good news about the changes is that she was able to stop taking a couple of medications per her doctor's orders.) As I was sitting at her kitchen table, trying to sort through them all, Lisa asked if I could make a colored mark on the medication list information sheet and use that same color to mark the medicine bottle. That way, anyone could pick up the paper, look at what was needed to fill the weekly pill bottles and find the corresponding container to finish the task. (I needed the markings and the color-coded system more than Lisa.) She just looks at the bottle, knows what it is, knows where she needs to put it in her cases and she can easily fill them herself. I love that I have been able to watch her become so capable with this important chore and seeing that she has it down systematically. She is definitely sure of herself and her knowledge about her medicines. She is definitely very competent and responsible when it comes to being in charge of her medications. It is unfortunate that Lisa has to take so much medication but I am grateful that those medicines are available for her to take. Hopefully, she can continue to do well maintaining her health with the help of the medications. I believe she can because she is organized, takes the medications as directed and knows facts about her medications. I think that is impressive.

CPAP

There were many times during Lisa's lifespan that I have worried about her health; times when I didn't know what to do or who to take her to; times when all I could do was worry or pray. I have heard it said, "Either worry or pray, but you can't do both." So, I alternated between the two, depending on the situation. Over the years, Lisa has been diagnosed with numerous health issues such as thyroid problems, sleep apnea, a vitamin deficiency and Sjogren's syndrome. And, oh yeah, she was diagnosed with Down syndrome at birth. I sometimes forget to include that in her repertoire of health concerns.

Lisa's first major health issue was when she was in seventh grade and she had been complaining of headaches. She also snored and seemed to sleep more and more. According to what the doctors told us about sleep apnea, Lisa only had a few of the 'at risk' factors, which were that her tongue seemed large for her small jaw bone and she had large tonsils. She had a sleep study done at the local hospital, but I don't remember much being said about the results. I don't believe they recommended anything except surgery. So at the age of 13, she had her tonsils and adenoids out. Lisa was treated to soft foods like popsicles, cold juices, mashed potatoes and puddings, and she recovered quickly from the surgery. She no longer snored and her headaches were gone. I thought that would be the end of it, but about ten years later she began to snore loudly again, so we took Lisa to a doctor for a check up on this matter. (Only later did I find a note Lisa had written in her school notebook, dated around this time that we were going to take Lisa to another doctor on this concern. The note said, "I am tired and dizzy, and I have a headache.") This new doctor decided that Lisa should have a polysomnography, otherwise know as a sleep study. At this time, Lisa was living in her own apartment. I took Lisa to the sleep center lab, filled out a bunch of insurance papers as well as noting Lisa's past history as it might pertain to her current complaints. She was assigned a private room and from what I could see, a very cushy bed. Lisa was very good while they hooked up all those wires, electrodes or sensors on her face and scalp. She had an oximeter sensor device on one of her fingers that measured the amount of oxygen in her blood and she had another item, like a belt, around her chest/abdomen area to measure her breathing. I believe they did an electrocardiogram (ECG) that recorded her heart rate and rhythm. There was other equipment in or around the room, but I wasn't sure what they were for. The staff that worked with Lisa were great, getting her to be still while they worked and getting her ready for a good night's sleep. I can't imagine how she could sleep with all those wires and other such things hooked up to her and to a machine. I was able to be with her while they worked, but at some point I was told it was time for me to leave.

    Before I left, I looked through a glassed area at her and saw that she was in bed, trying to get comfortable so she could sleep. I wondered how they would ever get her to the bathroom if she woke during the night needing to go, but that was not for me to be concerned about. The lab techs probably had encountered that situation plus many more issues in their time working at that facility. As it turned out, Lisa did fine. This sleep study showed that she had sleep apnea and it was recommended she use a CPAP machine at bedtime. CPAP is an acronym for "Continuous Positive Airway Pressure" and if test results come back positive for apnea, then that person needs to use a CPAP machine and wear a mask over either the nose or the mouth and nose while sleeping. The mask is hooked up to the machine and it delivers a continuous flow of air into the nose. I think Lisa started off with a mask over the mouth and nose, but in later testing, so the mask would be a good fit, she graduated to a nosepiece that only covers her nose. She has used that particular mask for over 12 years now and seems to work for her. About four years after this first sleep study, Lisa's cardiologist ordered a new study, partly because of Lisa's worsening sleep disorder and to be sure the CPAP was titrated properly. Titrate just means that the technicians will adjust the pressure needed for the person, and in this way the machine will be calibrated to the adequate pressure needed.

In Lisa's case, according to the final report, she was considered to have moderate obstructive sleep apnea, being severe at times. At her first sleep study, before she had the CPAP machine, she was having between 15-30 episodes of apnea an hour. That meant she stopped breathing that many times during the night while sleeping. She also had significant snoring episodes and mild hypoxemia, which meant she had an abnormally low level of oxygen in her arterial blood. Over all, she needed her machine recalibrated to meet her needs. She has had the air pressure settings changed twice, due to the study findings. She has been faithful in using the CPAP machine, and I am always taking note of when she complains of headaches, which isn't often or when she starts yawning more during the day. That's when I get with the doctor, who decides if she needs another sleep study done.

Using a CPAP machine can be frustrating for some, but for Lisa I think she adjusted quickly. Maybe it's because she felt better in the mornings, with no more headaches, snoring, being tired or acting moody. She is able to tolerate the gently forced air and seems to have the right fit for the mask and headgear. I believe she is comfortable sleeping with the equipment on and has no trouble falling asleep. I am sure that using her CPAP machine has been a plus when it comes to her overall health.

Eating And Exercise

For years I have been concerned about Lisa's weight gain. I first noticed it when she was having thyroid issues and I have since learned that weight gain is a definite symptom of hypothyroidism, which Lisa did develop. But, I think a lot of her weight gain was partly from the foods she chose to eat. The food choices and eating habits while she still lived at home were always pretty straightforward and basic. I called it "I cook it, you eat it" plan. I tried to have a balance of foods at each meal and no one ever went hungry, so I figured that was a good thing.

Everyone remembers the food pyramid, right? The triangle shaped sign that starts at the base showing vegetables, salad and fruit as the biggest portion of servings a day. From there, each tier has a different food group, from breads and pastas to dairy meats and oils. I won't go through all the details about this triangle, but this pyramid visual was a good tool to help me remember what we should be eating at each meal. The word 'should' is the optimum word, but I think the word 'could', should be a more reasonable word to use. So, I tried my best to instill good eating habits, with an occasional slip that ended up with us eating things that probably weren't on the healthy eating guideline list.

One of Lisa's biggest downfalls in the food department was anything sweet. She loved candy, sugary cereals, donuts, ice cream, ketchup, soda and flavored coffees. Just to name a few. She had little to no willpower, so when she was offered any of those things, she always accepted them with a smile. I know how difficult it is to be mindful of what to eat and not eat, so I could empathize with her. But, I also knew that I had to try to educate her on this topic of choosing the correct, healthy food and drink options because if she didn't monitor this closely, her chances of having diabetes would be almost inevitable.

When Lisa moved into her first apartment, I took her to the store when she needed groceries and I helped her to pick out things she could cook easily and still be somewhat healthy. I would try to change her mind when she wanted to buy a quart of ice cream or some other sweet treat. Then the realization came to me that she should be able to choose what she wanted at her apartment, because Lisa's dad and I have ice cream at our house, so why shouldn't she if that's what she wanted. I also felt that she was an adult and should be able to make her own choices, even though I would try to sway her from the ice cream to frozen yogurt or from the regular sodas to the diet sodas. I hoped to keep her weight down, but I realized that goal was not to be.

So, my next step was to give her information sheets that would help her to see all the good choices she could have when buying groceries or going out to eat. I found a lot of information on portion control and calorie count. One item I wanted to buy utilized a deck of cards, where you could pick cards from each food group and line them up each day so you knew what you were going to eat. (That is, if you had that food on hand.) I tried to explain this diabetic meal plan option to Lisa, but she never really seemed interested so I'm glad I didn't buy that. She didn't have diabetes either, but I thought the concept and food suggestions were good. The American Diabetes Association recommends four major food groups, vegetables, whole grains, low-fat dairy products and proteins. I printed out what I found on their website, read through it with Lisa and underlined what I thought was important to remember. Years later, I found this two-page print out stuffed in one of Lisa's folders that was hidden beneath a bunch of other folders and papers. Probably never looked at by Lisa again after I reviewed it so thoroughly with her years before.

My next tactic was to have picture prompts and a list of items that were acceptable to eat. These were suggestions about what fruits and vegetables to eat, what snack are acceptable and what items to avoid, like sugar products. I duplicated and plastered this clipping all over; on her frig with magnets or taped to the cupboards where she kept her food. I had some pictures that showed the proper portion size such as a three-ounce piece of meat would be about the size of a deck of cards or a small serving of a side dish like coleslaw would be the size of a computer mouse. You could have a potato if it was the size of a light bulb or a cup of rice could be the size of a tennis ball. I loved this idea of comparing sizes of food servings with an object you could relate to, because I could never visualize three ounces or what large or small sizes would look like. Another set of visual helps suggested was to use your hand. The fist would be considered about the size of a cup (8 ounces) or a medium fruit. The thumb, from the tip to the base would be about one ounce of meat or cheese or the cupped hand could be about one to two ounces of nuts. Again, I loved the visual because you always have your hand around to look at to compare how much of that meat or fruit you should really eat.

Twice we got Lisa a diet plate that was divided into sections. Both times we got this from a nurse practitioner in a hospital setting who worked with people who have Down syndrome. When Lisa got the first plate, the nurse practitioner explained the plate in detail, reading each section with Lisa and explaining how much of each food group should go into each divided section. Lisa did use the first plate for a while, but I think she probably piled the food high in each section, so that kind of defeated the purpose of the sections. That plate did get used but not for long. Then it stayed in Lisa's cupboard and finally got "lost," according to Lisa. The second time we got a plate, I wanted it out on the kitchen counter where she would see it even if she might not use it, but Lisa didn't have much counter space so I taped it to the wall, just above the top edge of the countertop. Every time I would go and visit, the plate would be on the counter so I thought maybe Lisa was using it, but she said, "No, it just keeps falling off the wall." I saw it on her table for a while but I think we ended up putting it in the cupboard where her other plates are stored, and I am sure she hasn't used it since.

There have been several successes in Lisa's attempts to lose weight. One time, she was a part of an eighteen-month program that was offered through our state university. The purpose was to compare two different diets and how these diets influence body weight and health. The difference between the diets was the use (or not) of prepackaged meals versus traditionally prepared meals. Lisa had to fill out a form and sign a release before starting the program. There was a person who visited with Lisa on a regular basis to discuss how she was doing, what she was eating and to check her weight. I do know that Lisa did lose weight and kept it off for a while. But, at some point the weight came back. Probably because Lisa had completed the program and was released from the spot checks and social calls from the person who had been visiting her throughout the course of the program. I kept all the information that was used with Lisa during that time and I tried to encourage Lisa to continue to follow what she had learned, but that didn't work so well. She soon returned to eating what she wanted and however much she wanted.

I tried to talk to Lisa about her weight and my concerns. When we went to a restaurant together, I would suggest that she try eating only half of what was served. Then she could ask for a box and take the other half home for another meal. Besides saving money when eating out, she was also saving on calories per meal. She did understand that, and now when we go out she will occasionally ask for a box. My only negative thought was that she probably only did that when she was out to eat with her dad and I, but I later learned otherwise. She would call me after she had been out to eat with friends, told me what she ordered and say, "I took half of it home so I have another meal tomorrow." And that made me feel good, knowing that she did get what I was trying to say.

Another part of the weight gain was her lack of exercise, so I tried to incorporate some into her daily routine. I would go over to her apartment and walk with her every morning for about fifteen to twenty minutes, which was about two times around her apartment building. This didn't last long because that was during the time when she was depressed and really didn't want to do anything except sleep. Later on, I would start to take her to one of our department stores and just walk around inside for twenty minutes or so. Lisa usually had something on her list that she wanted to buy and sometimes I did too. My trick was for us to walk to one section of the store, usually in the far corner of the store, and then I'd say something about being in the wrong part of the store. From there I might even say that I needed another item in a section of the store up front, so we'd walk up there to get what I needed. After that I might say something about going to look at t-shirts or jewelry, which would have us walking to yet another part of the store. I tried to keep this up as long as Lisa was willing to walk and sometimes this tactic worked great. Lisa's pace wasn't very quick, and it never has been. I remember a quote from one a doctor Lisa sees. We were talking about Lisa and her walking for exercise, and the doctor said, "Just remember. Lisa has two speeds; slow and stop."

If it was a nice day, I might suggest that we drive out to the lake and walk around a small pond that is part of the arboretum. We might have one walk around the pond before I saw that Lisa was slowing down. I'd ask if she wanted to go around again and most of the time her answer was no. But, once in awhile she might say yes and I'd have to make sure she meant it, because as I told her, "If you can't make it all the way around we would be stuck, because I can't carry you back to the car." I guess it was funny enough that she would laugh at my silly comment and then we would be off and walking around a second time.

There were other times when I would try to bribe her into walking. I would promise something if she would just walk ten more minutes. One offer was that she could have a certain t-shirt that she kept eyeing as we walked by it on our department store walks. The bribe would be that she had to walk three more times with me before she could have the t-shirt. T-shirts were always a big incentive for Lisa so I had to make sure I bought the t-shirt before it was sold out because I knew she would complete the challenge just to get that certain t-shirt she was promised. If she didn't walk those extras times as we had agreed on, then I'd save the t-shirt for the next bribe time. I don't know if this helped her lose weight but I think she was walking more often and now she doesn't get grouchy when I mention that we should go walk.

Maintaining weight can be a struggle, but for someone like Lisa, who has Down syndrome, hypothyroidism and a family history of diabetes, weight gain is difficult to avoid. She has several health factors that attribute to that weight, so maintaining or losing weight is always going to be a struggle. I know she has been given the right tools and information to make good judgments in this area, and I know that at times, she will try to do the best she can to help herself maintain healthy eating habits. And, this is all I can hope for.

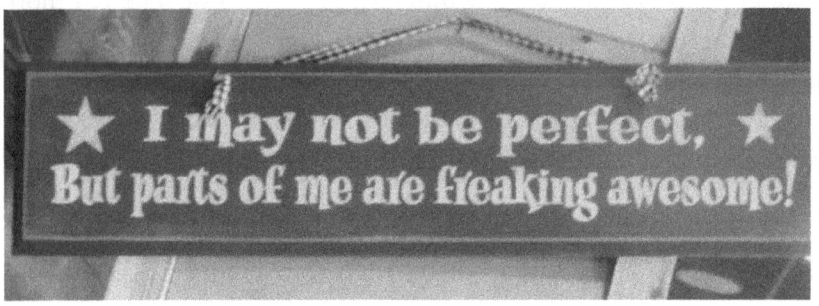

Voices And Depression

One of the worst times in regards to Lisa's health was when she started hearing voices. (And they weren't mine.) She had moved into her own apartment when she was twenty-two or twenty-three. She was happy, excited and very ready to be on her own. She did not want a roommate, except maybe a cat. She was finally fulfilling an IEP (Individual Educational Plan) goal from grade school. In her own words, those she had said many times, she wanted "to graduate from high school, get a job, live in my own apartment and own a cat." Well, she was on her way to most of those wishes. The cat would come later on, after she settled into her place and when I knew she was ready to care for another living creature.

The voices started very innocently. Lisa said she thought she heard her neighbor across the hall saying things and then later on Lisa said she thought it was the upstairs neighbor. This was a new set of circumstances for me and I truly didn't know where to go for help. Thank God we had a great mental health facility in town, and I scheduled an appointment for Lisa to see a psychiatrist. I wasn't sure how this would all work out, because it usually took Lisa a long time to warm up to someone before she would actually look at and talk to that person. (That was also a long-standing IEP goal: to look at the person in front of her, make eye contact and to talk to them.) She no longer has IEPs, but that was one goal we always had to work on.

The psychiatrist was very professional, and also personable in her interactions with Lisa on that first visit and on subsequent visits. Of course, in this current day and age, Lisa had to give permission for me to be with her in the room and that I could talk to the psychiatrist if needed. I tried to let Lisa talk as much as she wanted, which wasn't much most of the time. For that first visit, with most of the questions asked of her, Lisa would look at me and say "Mom" with a questioning look and her eyes dark with fear, as if her answers would be wrong. Then, I would answer the question with details that I remembered Lisa had told me. I always referred back to Lisa, asking her if that was true, if that is how she said it and did she have anything else to add. Over the years, yes, years that Lisa saw the psychiatrist, being uncertain of her answers was usually the norm. Occasionally, the doctor would ask Lisa to go into her office alone and that would make my radar go up immediately, at least in the beginning of this process. I worried about what Lisa might say that wasn't accurate or if the doctor would misconstrue what Lisa said and make more out of it than what really happened.

Early on in therapy, Lisa was given a baseline check that included answering questions to see if she was developing dementia. According to the Alzheimer's Association web site, there is no single test that proves that a person has Alzheimer's or related dementias. [7] Testing may include a physical exam and diagnostic tests, a neurological exam, a review of all medications taken and possibly lab tests. With a neurological exam, the doctor would test for such things as reflexes, coordination, eye movement, speech and sensory concerns that include feeling a light touch, pain and temperature.

With Lisa, her psychiatrist did a mental status test, and it was basically a series of questions to see about her mental skills. This was a simple set of questions, such as telling someone her address, what time it was and having to remember several words told to her, which she had to repeat later as a way of testing her cognitive function. I was concerned about these questions, because even though she knew how to tell time or knew how to remember words, I wasn't sure that she would respond to this person's questions appropriately. But, as I sat somewhat behind Lisa while she and the psychiatrist worked through the process, I was pleasantly surprised at how well she did with her responses. Maybe not always correctly, but close. That was good enough for me.

Visits to this psychiatrist were on a regular basis, first meeting every two weeks and then going once a month for sessions. At some point in time, in the early stages of her therapy, Lisa was put on a medicine called Abilify, the generic name being aripiprazole. This medication is usually used to treat specific mental health issues or mood disorders.[8] It can also be used to decrease auditory hallucinations, which is why Lisa was seeing the psychiatrist. Lisa began taking the smallest dose possible. Within weeks, Lisa reported that she no longer heard voices, so I gave a prayer of thanks, a sigh of relief and we went back to what I thought would be the easy, carefree world I had grown accustomed to with Lisa as an adult living on her own. A year went by, with the psychiatrist finally closing Lisa's case file because Lisa seemed to be doing fine. Lisa stayed on the medicine but soon she started to hear voices again. She was also more apathetic, quiet, withdrawn and simply not the easy-go-lucky, happy, funny daughter that I knew. It seemed like the spark in her eyes and her cheerfulness had vanished.

    I asked for and received the okay to have blood tests done. Lisa's blood levels showed that her B12 and thyroid levels were low. The family doctor had to increase both medication doses. The psychiatrist changed Lisa's medicine, too. Lisa started on a different medicine named Geodon and it was a stronger dose. This medication has the generic name of ziprasidone Hcl and it is also used to decrease hallucinations. It is considered an atypical antipsychotics medication, as was the first medication tried, Abilify. After Lisa started on the Geodon, she started to have more physical problems such as severe stomach upset, numbness in her hands and feet, dry skin and being very tired. I don't think this was related to her hearing voices and her depression, but these new complaints and symptoms seemed to materialize all at once. In the midst of all this, she had to have her gallbladder out. I thought this might be the culprit, but no, it was just another health issue to take care of. There was another increase in her Geodon, which didn't seem to help, because she was still hearing voices. Of course, all these things were adding to Lisa's stressors, both physically and mentally. The psychotropic medicines were being changed or the dosages increased, trying to get Lisa back to some kind of even keel in her health issues. Nothing was working and I was beside myself with worry over Lisa's mental state. I didn't know what was going on in her head, but on a good day she might tell me how she was feeling. She shared that she was concerned about her weight, she did not want to work very hard at her job and she did not like herself. This was definitely not the Lisa I knew. She had always had such good self-esteem and carried herself with such remarkable self-assurance and poise. I was at a loss and didn't know what I could do to help her.

Knowing what I know now, I think I should have seen at least some of the signs of depression. Some such symptoms include being tired, sleeping too much, feeling helpless, overeating and loss of interest in activities. Lisa displayed many of these symptoms. At first, she had trouble getting up and out of bed in the mornings, and I just thought she wasn't interested in going to work. I tried to help her by setting her alarm clock to ring in the morning. She had never really had to use an alarm before because she has an uncanny ability to just wake up at the correct time, no matter how early that might be. The alarm idea didn't work. Next, I scheduled a time in the morning for me to go over to her apartment to meet for a short walk before she had to go to the community day services program. We would make a few trips walking about her apartment building. I had hoped that by getting her moving, out of her apartment for some exercise and being able to spend time with me, it would help her mental and physical state. In the beginning, she was cooperating, but as the weeks wore on, she was less than enthused about the activity. I pushed back the walking to three days a week. She would walk, but her steps would be slow, deliberate and sluggish. Eventuality, I arrived at her place to do our walking activity, and she would not ready for me. She would still be in bed. I insisted that she at least try to walk with me, and she did so begrudgingly. So, this would be the new pattern. I would go over, she wouldn't be ready, I would wait, we'd walk a little and then she would be tired and quit. I finally told her that I would wait for her to call me, and we could walk whatever day she wanted. I had hoped that she would let me know when she wanted to resume the walking, but guess what, she didn't call. Technically, that was the end of that routine. But, what happened next was more troublesome to me.

When these new issues first began for Lisa, specifically her not being able to function in the morning, a transit bus that used to pick her up for work was temporarily cancelled, because she couldn't seem to be ready when they arrived. There were certain rules for being ready, and if not ready, there was a possibility of losing the privilege of riding. Because we cancelled the bus service, I would go over there to walk with her and afterwards, to take her to work. When I thought Lisa could handle getting on the bus in a timely manner, we had the bus schedule restarted so Lisa would have a ride. Then, I would get a call from Lisa's workplace saying that she had missed the bus. I would go over to her apartment only to discover that she was still in bed at 10 a.m., which is just not something Lisa had ever done before. She was always an early riser, always on time for her bus and hardly ever missed going to work. So, my newest morning schedule was to go over there, let myself into her apartment, get Lisa up, have her get ready for work, and then take her there. (I was feeling like I was being duped, and that I was also enabling her.) Either way, it was not a good situation. I also goofed by saying things like, "You can't stay in bed all morning," "You can't be that tired" or "You need to be responsible". When someone is depressed, this is not what you say. But, at this time, I had not put it together that she was depressed. I just thought she was getting lazy.

More medicines, more visits to the psychiatrist, more issues to handle. And, the scary, breaking point for Lisa and I was when the doctor said Lisa was having thoughts of suicidal ideation. This means that a person is thinking about suicide, but the range of feelings could include a single, brief thought to severe thoughts of wanting to commit suicide. This is when I leaned on God's steady hand and the psychiatrist's advice. Lisa's dad and I had to take Lisa to another city to admit her to a psychiatric unit. It was one of the darkest days of my life with Lisa. I remember gathering up a small suitcase of Lisa's clothing, medicines and other overnight articles that she might need. And, I had a difficult time as I tried to put on a good front for Lisa's sake. I explained that it would only be for a little while, so the staff of nurses and doctors could help her through this rough time. I told her that they would be able to care for her, talk to her, have her in more counseling sessions and help her to feel better. What happened was that they kept her there three nights and two days, increased one of her medicines and added another and monitored her activities, which were very few. I remember when we took her there; we filled out the paperwork and got a quick tour of where her room was and where the cafeteria was. We were told that she would have group and individual sessions. Each time Lisa asked me why she was there, I'd have to explain it to her again, each time I visited. I now feel that she should not have been there. The staff related to us that she didn't talk to anyone. Hum, I could have told them that would happen. She didn't do any activities except watch television. Hum, I could have told them that would happen, too. But, she did start something new while she was there. She started tearing her hair out in clumps. More than once this was reported to me, but at no time was there anyone telling me that they tried to stop her or to help her.

Lisa was released with more medications but little else. I don't think that was a good move on our part to have sent her there, but at the time we thought that might help Lisa and keep her safe. We brought her back home, trying to decide what else we could do. She had visits with the psychiatrist, and Lisa's Geodon antipsychotic medicine kept being increased. Lisa kept hearing voices, and not just at her apartment. We would take her out for a meal, and she would not like the loud restaurant noises. She would hold her head and complain about the noise and the voices. When I asked her about them, she would mention a woman's name and say that person was bothering her in her head, but she couldn't understand what the woman was saying to her. Lisa was crying, asking why the lady was doing that to her. Lisa said it was scary, and that she was afraid she might have to go back to the psychiatric unit again. I reassured her that I would not let that happen again. Of course, I didn't know what other options we might have to help Lisa, but I knew I didn't want her back at that facility either. It had been three years since Lisa first started on antipsychotic medications, and there was no improvement in Lisa. In fact, it was so much worse than I could ever have imagined. So, I did a little research, using my old nursing books, and came up with a solution that I thought might work.

At the next visit to the psychiatrist, I asked that Lisa be taken off her antipsychotic medications. I also wanted Lisa to consult with a counselor on a regular basis, because I felt that such a change might make a difference. So, over a course of three to four months, Lisa got off the medicines. I watched her carefully and talked about the voices on occasion, to see if she had any new voices that bothered her. Most of the time she would report that she didn't hear any voices, but occasionally she would admit that the woman would bother her, especially in the evening. So, I asked Lisa what she did about hearing the voices and Lisa said, "I just tell her to be quiet." I guess that helped because over time Lisa would say that she didn't feel depressed, she became more talkative, happier and even had a quicker pace to her walking. When her fear faded, so did mine.

BARCUS

Medical Record Keeping

Once Lisa started to have many more medical needs, I had a lot of papers about those needs that I needed to file in some kind of orderly fashion. I got out a large three-ring binder to keep all that pertinent information in one place. I guess I'm just a little whacky about things like that, but this binder has saved me a few times, especially when I quickly needed some health information about Lisa.

On the outside of this black binder there is a clear, plastic cover and it protects the front and back of the binder. This has come in handy because I would usually place different items in the front sleeve that I wanted to remember when Lisa would have a doctor's appointment, such as the lab requisition that Lisa would need to have done when we arrived at the doctor's office. Other times it might be a note to tell the front office staff of a new insurance for Lisa or when I needed to update her medical files with a new medicine or diagnosis. But, the best items I've put in that front sleeve of the binder have been several different photos of Lisa. One is at her highest weight when she was on some psychotropic medicines, one when she lost quite a bit of weight and she was off those medicines and a third photo shows her where she is at now with her weight.

You can see a distinct difference in the weight changes and I show that to doctors who haven't seen her for a while or maybe at a first visit with a new doctor, especially when they mention her weight. It's a big, ongoing issue and Lisa tries her best when she is making her food choices, but the weight is such a struggle. So, showing the doctors the different pictures gives them a different perspective about Lisa and her weight issues.

On the inside of the front and back covers there is a half side pocket which I utilize by putting information that is needed for almost every doctor visit Lisa goes to. I keep her current medication list in the front pocket, along with a few older lists of her past medications. On these sheets I have listed the medication, when it was first prescribed, by whom, dosage and how many times a day it is taken, what the color and shape of the tablet is and the reason why she takes the medicine. This helps me so I don't have to remember all the medications Lisa takes or has taken. Lisa does a great job remembering the names of the meds, what they look like and why she takes them. When I say something like, "You know, that medicine you take for your thyroid problem," and she'll say something like, "Oh, the levothyroxin." Or I will ask her about a certain medicine, usually saying the generic name, and she will respond with the correct diagnosis for why she is taking that medicine. Along with the current medication list, I have made another med list that is set up to show all her meds in the order she takes them during the day, listing first the morning meds, then the noon meds, after work meds and then the night time meds. I also jot down what color and shape each pill container is, and this is especially helpful for me if I ever go over and help her organize her medications for the week. I think I actually did this for me so I can check her work, and for any other staff person or family member who might just have to help Lisa with her medications when I'm not around. For years she has filled her own pill containers and does exceptionally well with that task. Lisa even came up with the idea to color code the medication bottles and the medication sheet, so that she knows she is filling the medications correctly in the containers. Lisa gave me some colored pencils she had and she picked out some of the brighter colors to use. Then I colored in a small circle on each pill bottle and used that same color to do a circle next to that medicine as it is listed on the sheet. Thanks, Lisa. That was a really smart idea!

The back pocket of the three-ring binder has her insurance information as well as the pharmacy medication information sheets that we get each time Lisa has a medication filled. The pharmacy sheet tells everything you'd ever want to know about the medicine, like the brand name and generic name, how to use the medicine, any side effects, precautions when using the medicine, drug interactions, overdose procedure and other notes. This has come in handy when I want to look up something about the medicine and don't want to Google it. There are ten tabs for this binder, sometimes combining several different topics under one tab heading.

Tab one has information on the different diagnoses that Lisa has and specific information for those less common diagnoses, such as Sjogren's or B12 deficiency. There is also information on some of the medications that Lisa takes in relationship to the diagnosis, some information I knew from personal experience and other information from a website of the disorder in question. Again, it is for my benefit as well as others who might have to access the information on Lisa's health issues.

Tab two is about Down syndrome. Yes, you can't ever know too much about Down syndrome, especially if you have a child with Down syndrome. Some of this information covers visits that Lisa has had with a medical person who is an Advanced Practice Registered Nurse and works specifically with people who have Down syndrome. I have also included Lisa's pertinent health history involving her different aliments and diagnoses. I have a form that shows how to screen for dementia, which is a concern for those who have Down syndrome. Some information that is included is specifically about people with Down syndrome and the incidence of dementia. The information I have printed off shares some statistics that show evidence of people with Down syndrome being at an increased risk for dementia. And, most people with Down syndrome will probably face some brain changes as they get older, but not everyone will have Alzheimer's or dementia.

Tab three has Lisa's labs that are done on a yearly basis, as well as other labs that might be done every three to six months to be sure those labs are stable. I have also utilized this section to keep any x-rays or magnetic resonance imaging (MRI) that have been done.

Tab four is her cardiology section. In addition to having the written report from her yearly visit, I also ask the technician if I can have a copy of the electrocardiogram (EKG or ECG). This is a simple, noninvasive technique that allows doctors to check for signs of heart disease. The results show the heart rhythm, if there is poor blood flow to the heart muscle, if there has been a heart attack and any other abnormalities. [9] I also have a running list of the times Lisa has visited the nurse at her workplace to have her blood pressure taken. This information is useful to the cardiologist and other doctors, because the results of the blood pressure ranges show how or if the medication is helping to keep her blood pressure in a good, healthy range.

Tab five has information from several different doctors. One is her kidney specialist, another is her nephrologist and the third is her rheumatologist, who monitors Lisa problems associated with her having Sjogren's syndrome. I receive the written reports from each visit, and if there is any lab work done I have that filed there, too. This section is also where I keep the information we have when Lisa has had a polysomnograph, which is a sleep study. Lisa has had this done at least three times so far. It was initially done because of her complaints of being tired, having headaches and her snoring.

Tab six is a grab bag of items. I have a current list of Lisa's health conditions, which I usually update through Lisa's family practice doctor and their on-line access to Lisa's medical information. I also check Lisa's health insurance company's website that lists all her health issues, current and past conditions. I have noted the major health problems, listing when they were first diagnosed and what was done for treatment. I have a one-page summary of the family medical history, from both sides of the family. In this summary, I list the diagnosis, who had or has it, and if there was or is a treatment plan.

Other papers such as proof of guardianship, medical release forms or eye doctor information might also be in this section.

Tab seven deals specifically with Lisa's past problems in conjunction with depression, some information on the subject, some related issues Lisa had due to having depression, as well as a seven-page overview of depressive disorders in adults with Down syndrome that I felt had some very useful information.

Tab eight deals with Lisa's current medications. I keep at least six months of those lists in this binder, so I can refer back to an older sheet to jog my memory of why a medication was prescribed or discontinued. I think I use this section often because if there is a slight change in a medication, I need to update it. I keep the old sheet behind the newest sheet for a while, so I can access the older information if needed.

Tab nine is a single sheet that contains Lisa's personal medical history, which has all her pertinent information that I might need when going to the doctor or to have some labs drawn. (Yes, it's a single sheet, but the font size is very tiny). I have her family practice doctor and her cardiologist listed at the top, along with their phone numbers, in case someone needs to get ahold of one of them quickly. This sheet briefly mentions previous illnesses and surgeries and her problems at birth with her heart. It also has several other medical issues that are more relevant than some of her lesser medical problems. I have her current immunizations on this sheet, because I got tired of trying to find the little booklet we had used when she was younger that had the immunizations listed. I have a section on what doctor she had recently seen, the date and reason for the visit and any remarks that might be necessary to note. There is a small section where I might write a note that I want to remember to ask a doctor a specific question. There is space in the margins for me to make notes whenever I take Lisa to the doctor. To update this sheet, I pull up the most current personal medical history form I have on my flash drive, where I add the new information from that doctor visit, using the information that came from the notes I wrote in the margins. Then I file this new sheet in front of all other doctor visit sheets under this specific tab.

Tab ten is basically any other papers that I thought were good information that related to something with Lisa, but didn't really fit under any of the other tabs. Whew!

This system works for me, because Lisa has had lots of health issues in her lifetime, and I just can't remember all of them all of the time. I like to be organized. I can go with Lisa to any doctor visit and be ready for anything question that might come up. One time, when Lisa had stomach issues that turned out to be gallbladder problems, the surgeon wanted to do an EKG before agreeing to do the surgery. I said I had one that was just done a few weeks before, so he looked at that and said, "That works." We didn't have to have a second one done, so we saved time and money. Another time, Lisa's family practice doctor was talking about some lab that Lisa had a few years before and the doctor asked if I remembered when that was done so she could look at the lab results in their computer system. Well, I think we had a race to see who could find the lab first, and I won. I was able to flip to the lab section and I found the lab report she was looking for and I found it faster than the doctor did using the computer. That was fun! Some of the information I have compiled about Down syndrome and related health issues has also come in handy. There were times when I quoted from specific articles I have in the binder or had read about elsewhere, and the doctor was gracious enough to listen and respond by saying that the information was interesting and that she would also look into it. I hope that I am able to enlighten others, so that others with Down syndrome have the best care and treatment possible, no matter what their health concern might be. Am I a little too organized or outlandish about my record keeping? I suppose so. My weirdness for organization extends beyond Lisa's three-ring binder. One such funny story is how I put my tissues in my coat pocket. The cleaned, unused ones go in my left-hand pocket and the used ones to throw away are in my right-hand pocket until I find a wastebasket. It's okay if you are laughing. I just have to be organized. In the case of the three-ring medical records binder, I feel it is what I need to do to help keep Lisa healthy and to keep me from always trying to find out where I put that important piece of paper. It works for me.

Vehicles

Of all the things I could have possibly thought of about Lisa's capabilities, I never would have added driving to the list. Granted, when she was little she was able to maneuver a tricycle, a big wheel and the small kiddie car rides that you see at the local fair. But, to think of Lisa actually driving something that was gas or electric powered was not a good thought for me. She did not have good reaction time to sudden movements nor did she have good vision. I think both attributes are a must when driving.

So when our grown children were sitting around the table sharing stories of things they had done with Lisa in years past, the story of Lisa driving her brother's car made me sit up and listen. This was a story I had not been told before. I think her older brother was telling his version, which included taking Lisa to the school parking lot near our home when Lisa was about fifteen or sixteen. She didn't have a driver's license or a permit to drive. The story goes that she was able to drive the car in that large school parking lot a few times and seemed to like it.

The next sibling to share a long remembered story was Lisa's other brother who revealed a similar story. When Lisa was maybe twenty-six, she was given another chance to drive again, probably because she had asked him if she could drive. Her reaction time and vision concerns were still issues to be aware of but that didn't stop her brother from giving her the opportunity to try again. I don't know how she did either time, but I suspect that if she had any mishaps during her driving experiences with her brothers, they would have let me know. Well, maybe not. I think kids will always be kids and they don't always 'fess up to things that went wrong during their growing up years.

After hearing about these stories of Lisa driving, I looked into the possibility of her taking a driver's class and the written test. I looked up all the possible arrangements that might have to be made for someone who had a developmental or intellectual disability. According to the Disability Driving Instructors site, if a person has learning difficulties, problems with reading or writing or might need additional help taking exams, that person might be able to receive some specific help. That could include having extra time to take the test, complete a spoken test via the computer, have a private environment/separate room to take the test or have a person who would read the questions word for word and then record the answer the candidate gave to the person helping the hopeful driver. Another suggested option was the Oral Language Modification (OLM), which meant the reader could explain the language meaning by rewording the questions to make them easier to understand. [10] In order to utilize some of the above-mentioned ways to receive the assistance, arrangements must be made when booking for the test.

According to the Safe Driving for Life website, "the driving test for those with disabilities won't be any 'easier' than it would be for a person who doesn't have a disability. You still have to take a 'test of competence to drive', which means that you'll have to show you're capable of controlling a car and following the rules of the road." [11]

With all that information, I contemplated the decision of whether to let Lisa try or explain to Lisa why I thought it was best if she didn't drive. I decided to talk with Lisa. We had a good talk, where I mostly talked and she listened. She had some good questions and I hope I had honest and satisfactory answers. Lisa contemplated all I had told her and commented by saying, "I think it is okay if I don't drive. You take me where I need to go anyway." I wasn't just looking after Lisa's safety but also of those on the road who might encounter Lisa and her driving.

That was the end of her wanting to drive a car but she did continue to drive on occasion. She has been out to the golf course a couple of times and drove a golf cart. I remember the first time she drove the cart. Lisa started the golf cart using the key for the electric cart, and then she pushed the accelerator. This made the cart jump forward quickly and it startled Lisa. I guess the accelerator was sensitive, so I tried to tell her to just put a little pressure on the pedal to get started and to get used to how much pressure was needed. She gradually got the hang of how forceful she should press down on the pedal to get the cart to move smoothly. (Thank goodness we were on flat ground when this lesson started or we probably would not have continued. I can't imagine what would have happened to Lisa and I if we had suddenly careened downhill with a definite possibility of a crash at the end.) As it was, Lisa was able to drive on the golf cart path at a very nice speed, using the brake when needed. She figured out that she could just let up on the gas and that would slow us down. She learned to slow down when turning on the curves and how to avoid running into a tree or bush. She got pretty brave over time and started taking the downhill slopes rather quickly. Most of the time I just held on tight and said very little. She was very conscientious about her driving and kept a sensible speed. After the group was finished with their round of golf, we headed back to the clubhouse. Lisa had one question for me, "When can I do that again?"

Lisa was also able to drive a 4-wheeler, thanks to one of my sisters who had such a vehicle and she allowed the nieces and nephews to ride when they came to visit her at her farm. I was a little concerned with letting Lisa go out with her cousins, but I really had no real reason to be. They all took turns driving and probably helped Lisa by telling her a few intricate details about driving a 4-wheeler. (Or at least I hope they helped her.) My other concern was that I couldn't see her at all times. Lisa's cousins, nieces and nephew would take turns driving, usually having two or three others with them in the vehicle. They would go up to the barn, down to the mailbox near the main road or around the orchard. I was always glad when I saw Lisa waiting near the house for her turn, because that was the only time I knew for sure where she was and that she was safe. I am so glad that she had this time to enjoy with family, and was able to do some more driving.

There was one car incident that no one expected. Lisa and her older brother decided to go on an outing. They drove to an area where there was a playground, a winding river, trees, ducks and other wildlife. It was a quiet, outdoor park setting. I'm not sure what Lisa and her brother did there, but I seem to remember that at one point Lisa's brother left the car for a short run while Lisa stayed in the car. When he returned, he said she wasn't in the car. He looked around the car and across the playground area, searching for Lisa. He finally found her in the trunk of the car. It was a hatchback with a cloth cover over the luggage area. Lisa was hiding under the lightweight, flexible material that was snapped in place and was used to keep people from seeing into that back area of the vehicle. Lisa's brother was not a happy camper. All Lisa said was she thought it would be funny to hide.

Lisa's driving days might be behind her, so she will have to be content to ride with someone. When she rides with me she is aware of the other cars and has comments about their driving habits. She will look to the side mirror on the passenger side, and might say something about the driver behind us being too close. This has always been a concern with her, even when I felt like the vehicle behind us was not that close. I think Lisa may be correct and that my ability to gauge how near the vehicle is behind us might not be as accurate as I believe. There was one Sunday when Lisa saw a driver who cut in front of a vehicle ahead of us, and she called him a sinner because he was a mean driver. Sometimes, Lisa will make a comment about motorcycle drivers, especially when she sees that a driver isn't wearing a helmet. The best comment I remember is, "No helmet.

That's just crazy. That's how people get their brain scrambled, sunny side up."

Our town has a bus transit system that has many designated stops along a regular route. Lisa has used this bus system on occasion, but most of the time she uses the transit system's door-to-door bus service, which is called a para-transit service or the T-Lift. In order to use this service, Lisa had to fill out some forms because there are certain eligibility requirements in order to qualify for the service. These forms also have to be updated every three years. There is a policy manual that has information about what is expected of the bus driver, pickup and drop off times, as well as the window of waiting times for both the driver and the rider before one is considered late.

The form had questions about a person's abilities and whether they were temporary or permanent. Because Lisa was born with Down syndrome, this is considered permanent. Other questions ask about a person's ability to cross a street, with help or on their own, if the person might have issues or problems when the weather changes, if the person could identify the correct bus and if the person needed a care attendant.

The first time Lisa used the service to go to work, I helped her schedule her ride by having her call in and I listened to her ride request. For her first call, she dialed the number and told the dispatch person that she needed a ride to her workplace. She had no other information, such as her address where they were to pick her up, the address where she was to be dropped off and no time requests. She had to hang up, discuss the information in detail with me and call again. Lisa finally got her first week of bus service scheduled and she was very proud of that. When I told her I'd be over on that first morning to make sure she got her ride, she said I didn't need to do that. She was very adamant that she was going to do it by herself. I was concerned with her getting to work, and waited nervously until the time that she was to arrive at work. That's when I knew she did it, because she didn't call me for a ride to get to work.

According to the bus service handbook, if the rider is late getting to the bus or doesn't cancel the ride before a certain time, there could be consequences and the rider might not be able to utilize the bus services for a while. Overall, Lisa has been able to learn the ropes of this door-to-door bus service and it has been very useful, as she needs rides to get to work at least six days out of the week. She is very responsible about making sure she is ready in plenty of time so the bus driver doesn't have to wait for her. Most of the time she is ready and waiting, sometimes inside her apartment, looking out the window or door for her ride, sometimes sitting outside on the front door steps. If the driver is late she will call their central office and ask about where the driver might be, so she knows how soon the bus will arrive. There have been a few 'on time' versus 'late incidences', but those are quickly resolved when the story of the guilty party explains the situation that may have caused the lateness. Having the bus transit system available has been very useful for Lisa and many others like her who need daily transportation to continue to be as independent as possible. I am so glad that Lisa lives in a great city that provides such a great service.

Preferred Lifestyle Plan, BASIS And Letter Of Intent

When Lisa was a newborn, we learned what an IEP entailed. This is an Individual Educational Plan and it was written up with Lisa in mind, telling of her educational needs and the services that would be provided by the school. As parents, we were part of the process of identifying the needs and services but really knew very little about the procedures of an IEP meeting or the significance of our comments. She was just a baby; what could she really do and what could help with her growth and development in the early months? Well, we found out fairly quickly. The first meeting was overwhelming because we didn't know what to expect, but it was good to know Lisa's strengths and weaknesses, and what the school system and teachers were going to do to help Lisa.

When Lisa finished her classroom schooling and moved on to adult services and supports, she still had yearly updates that were called a Preferred Lifestyle Plan or a Circle of Support. Somewhere along the way, I called it a Person-Centered Plan, though I don't have any saved documents that show what the plan was really named. That title may have come from one of the other states we had lived in or I heard the phrase from someone else. I don't really know what the plan is now called but when we have a yearly meeting, the plan that the professional staff uses seems to be the same, discussing services, supports and other pertinent information that others need to know about Lisa. So I continue to call it a Person-Centered Plan. And, really, what's in a name anyway. The review of this plan starts with an overview of Lisa, her goals and progress. This states where she lives, where she works and what social activities she participates in. There is a description of a typical day and an ideal day, with information from us parents, from Lisa and others who work with her as well. There is a list of things she has done in the past year, such as going to a WWE live wrestling events or to another state for a week's vacation with family. And just recently, there was an added section for Lisa to have a goal, something that Lisa has to agree to and that would be relevant to her needs. It could be something like "maintaining a healthy diet," "reducing a behavior issue" or some other such meaningful or reachable goal.

The pages go on to list her residential preferences, work preferences, social activities, religious preference and other topics. I describe how to best communicate with Lisa, and I share her health information as well as any personal and financial information that might be important. I have always believed that this plethora of information is important, so others might know more about Lisa, her strengths, interests, needs and wants. It helps to have a plan for her future, to assure that if we are not around, Lisa will be able to continue life without too much change. Lisa is always there in attendance to hear the comments and updates, and she has a part in the decision-making that is very important to her independence and how she lives. Each state may have a different form they use, but I think the concept is pretty much the same. It is a good tool to use and follow, and I am glad we had this as part of Lisa's plans for the future.

Another yearly review that Lisa has is called a BASIS Assessment. This tool was developed as an evaluation test to help determine the level of support for an individual's needs. Prior to the BASIS, there was no standard as to how to determine a tier level for someone. A tier level is a rating system to decide reimbursement rates to pay for services needed. The BASIS is used to determine and maintain eligibility for people who utilize a waiver program called the Home and Community Based Services (HCBS). Information comes from those who work with Lisa, as well as others who may have input on her behaviors and daily living skills. Of course, Lisa's dad and I are a part of this data gathering as well. This material is compiled and entered into a database. The results are then scored, and from that the state gives a tier score, which impacts Lisa plan of care and her need for Home and Community Based services (HCBS). Again, each state has different types of services available, different yearly assessments required and different options. So, depending on where someone lives, there are probably some similar yearly evaluations in place.

Our form has a basic information page, listing pertinent data about Lisa, such as name, birthday, address and identified disability. There is a medical assessment, based on a review with Lisa and myself, as well as any doctors documentation and other information gathered by the staff at the agency where she works. There is a page about mobility, if she can do simple requests like telling time, if she can do simple addition, if she understands simple directions and if she can relate experiences when asked. These are just a few of the topics that are covered. They have a page on behaviors and it is detailed with such line items as: Does she have tantrums? Is she self-injurious? This page also wants to know if she can brush her hair or choose appropriate clothing for the changing weather, as well as wanting to know how independent she is in making her bed or doing laundry, plus other such pertinent pieces of information.

The first time I sat through a meeting like this was somewhat perplexing. I wasn't sure why they needed to know so much personal information and yet I knew that the answers were important to her receiving the needed services and funding that would be available to her. I now look at it as a way for the state to have a checks and balance system, to be sure that Lisa still qualifies for services and is getting what she needs. It seems to me that the Person Centered Plan and the BASIS have similar questions and concerns so I don't understand why there are so many questions, forms and paper. It would be nice if the two could be combined into one, but I believe they are required by the state, from two different agencies. So, we continue to duplicate to appease those yearly requirements.

As long as we are on the topic of Lisa's needs, there is another bit of information that I found very useful. It's called a Letter of Intent and we first heard about this when we went to a lawyer to have our wills updated. He was someone who dealt with families who had a child with special needs, and seemed to be very knowledgeable. I was given some information about how to start, but I like to think that I improved on the idea by adding other items every year when I updated Lisa's letter. Our Letter of Intent spells out specific, vital information about Lisa, in case someone else is taking care of her, whether it is one of her older siblings or the support staff that have worked with her over the years. I update, copy and save the Letter of Intent, then copies are sent to her siblings and our lawyer. I do this yearly, trying to stay on top of any major changes that have happened and new topics or information that I feel might be useful to know. I list family members and medical information. These topics spread out over nine pages, and I get very detailed in some areas, mentioning the different doctors she sees and how to reach them. I even write less important things like what type of toothbrush and toothpaste she uses or how she reacts at eye doctor appointments. I mention her health insurance plans, medications she takes and the diet plan she should have as opposed to the diet she would rather follow. I relate her housing situation, where she has lived in the past and what she wants as far as any living arrangements for now and in the future. I list the furniture and household items that she has or owns. I tell about her current activities, what she may need as far as working on her self-help skills and domestic activities, her capabilities with handling money, getting public transportation and other skills necessary to survive independently. I specifically mention information pertinent to caregivers, their attitudes, how they should handle conversing with her because of her hesitance to respond quickly and the need to encourage her with positive comments to help with self-esteem. I comment on her sleep habits, personal finance and her need for an allowance. I list brand names of clothes that work well for Lisa and even mention specific stores that have a better selection for her body shape. I mention what types of clothes she likes to wear and what she doesn't or won't wear. I recount her past education and current support services. I tell of her work history, her likes and dislikes and what to expect for any future employment positions. I describe her leisure and recreational activities, as well as the organizations that she is a member of and is active in. I mention her religious background and what Lisa, her dad and I want in this regard as well. I go in to detail about Lisa's rights and values, summing up how she should be able to maintain an active life, be a contributing member of the community, have meaningful work, be directed in handling money appropriately and to live as independently as possible with supports as needed. I end the Letter of Intent with our intentions for Lisa, stating that she should be given every opportunity to live and be included as a member of the community, to equally share in and enjoy with others the values of family, faith, friends, health, love, work and financial security.

My hope is that with all the detailed information I have put in this Letter of Intent, anyone who ends up caring for Lisa after our death can do so without too much of a disruption in Lisa's routine and life. No one knows Lisa as well as her dad and I do. We want others to know what works best for Lisa and to give them what they need to make it the best for Lisa. I want to minimize any disruption that may occur when we die or if we are unable to care for her. I want her to feel comfortable around those who are caring for her. I cherish the people who work with her and support her in her daily activities now and I hope that the supports for Lisa can continue long after we are gone.

Special Needs Trust And ABLE Accounts

When we went to our lawyer to have our wills and estate plans drawn up, we were encouraged to also have a special needs trust set up for Lisa, to be funded at the time of our death. We were told about a special needs trust but there is also a similar option called supplemental needs trust (SNT.) According to Margolis & Bloom, LLP there is really no difference between these two mentioned trusts. "The term, 'special' needs trust refers to the purpose of the trust to pay for the beneficiary's unique or special needs. In short, the title is focused more on the beneficiary while the name 'supplemental' needs trust addresses the shortfalls of our public benefits programs." [12]

These trust funds are set up so a person with a disability remains eligible for government benefits and can use funds from the trust for things not covered by government benefits. Expenses such as hiring a personal care attendant, going on vacation, paying for dental or other medical expenses not covered through insurance plans or to buy a vehicle for personal use. The trust is written with the person in mind, and it allows that person to benefit from the available funds without compromising their other government benefits. A trust can contain cash or other assets as well as personal property that can be turned into cash. Mixing government benefits and personal funding is complicated. My best suggestion would be to seek professional, legal advice.

A trust is a legal arrangement where one party has control of property for the benefit of another. Property may include cash, personal and/or real estate property. There are several different types of special needs trust funds, and I cannot say I know all the options. Again, find someone, like a lawyer or a financial advisor who is skilled in this area to help set up a trust. In the case of someone who receives Social Security Income (SSI), a discretionary trust means the SSI beneficiary doesn't have control on how the money is used and another person, a trustee, takes care of or manages the trust and makes decision in regards to how the money is spent. Money or property held in a trust for someone who benefits from SSI doesn't count toward the SSI limits of $2,000 that an individual is limited to. But, some trusts may affect Medicaid eligibility.

There are some regulations that come into play about how to set up a trust, and one such regulation has to do with supplemental Security Income (SSI). This government program assists people with low incomes who have special needs. One of the qualifications for SSI was that Lisa could only have $2,000 in money or assets. One of the main reasons someone would want to set up a special needs trust would be if that person has a possibility of acquiring more money or assets, such as an inheritance or gifts, valued above the capped amount of $2,000. If a person goes over that amount, they risk the chance of losing other benefits such as health care and housing assistance. Some things needed by a person with special needs are not covered by medical insurance, Medicare or Medicaid. So, the special needs trust is a way to have other monies to be used for that person's benefit. You must also be aware that some trusts that are not counted as resources for some organizations such as SSI, may affect other programs such as Medicaid eligibility. You will have to check with a lawyer in the state you are living in to be sure this won't have an impact on the Medicaid eligibility. With some types of trusts, when that person dies, the remainder in the trust would be given to a government program such as Medicaid for the cost of past medical care benefits received from that government program.

This topic is a difficult one to explain and to write about clearly. Partly because every person who has special needs has different needs and that means the trusts would be individualized for each person. Lisa's special needs trust is not funded until her dad and I are both deceased. Then, a portion of the money from our estate would go into her special needs trust, which would then be managed by a person we named to that position of "trustee" for the special needs trust. This person has specific duties to fulfill on Lisa's behalf for the management of the trust fund. The trustee will manage this for as long as it is needed or until the funds run out. Lisa's trustee can use the money on items that are necessary for Lisa's benefit, so she can continue to have her basic needs met and live without hardship.

There is a tax-advantaged saving account for people with disabilities and their families, called the ABLE account, which was established by the Achieving Better Life Experience act of 2014. According to their website, "the beneficiary of the account is the account owner, and income earned by the accounts will not be taxed.

Contributions to the account, which can be made by any person (the account beneficiary, family and friends) must be made using post-taxed dollars and will not be tax deductible for purposes of federal taxes, however some states may allow for state income tax deductions for contribution made to an ABLE account." [13] This is a way to save extra money and still stay within the limitation of only having $2,000 in assets.

The reason for the ABLE accounts has to do with the fact that most people who have a disability have to depend on programs that help them with their food, housing and health care, to name a few. And, to remain eligible for these benefit programs a person cannot exceed the $2,000 assets limit. Any savings they might want to have could possibly affect their benefits from resources such as Medicaid, Section 8 Housing or SSI.

To be eligible for the ABLE account, the person with a disability must have been diagnosed before the age of 26. There are also some other parts to the eligibility that have to do with receiving benefits through SSI or SSDI. SSDI is Social Security Disability Income and SSI is Supplemental Security Income. To me, this is somewhat confusing, what with all the acronyms being used, but one of the good things about an ABLE account is that the person with the account can actually have up to $15,000 given to them in one year. Then, this can be repeated yearly, up to a certain amount. I read that some states have set limits as to how much can be in the ABLE account; some limits are around $300,000. This all sounds pretty good for the person with the disability, because they can save money to be used for their needs without losing the government funding they might be receiving. There are certain expenses listed that the ABLE account can be used for. Some of these expenses are not covered by other benefit programs (government programs) and could include such things as the cost of housing, transportation, personal support services, assistive technology items and other such needs that could help the person's quality of life or to allow them greater independence. And, it doesn't matter what state you live in. You may enroll in another state's ABLE program if they are willing to accept you as an out of state resident. [14]

It's important when setting up a trust fund to say the trust is for extra care or supplemental needs beyond what the government provides and that the trust is not to be considered a basic support trust. [15] There are other suggestions and possible language to use, to make sure the trust is used as it has been intended. There are many websites with good information on this topic and I am sure there are many lawyers who are well versed in special needs trusts. It is important to search out all the options so you have a wide view of what is available and what might be the most appropriate way to help in securing the best for your child. My head is spinning with all this jargon. I hope I didn't make this too confusing.

BARCUS

Useful Information On Benefits And Assistance Programs

Before Lisa was born, we were not handed a book or booklet that would tell us everything we would have to know about raising a child with Down syndrome. With Lisa's older siblings we weren't handed a book either, but I had the book "The Common Sense Book of Baby and Child Care" by Dr. Benjamin Spock. His first book was written in 1946 and its message to mothers was that "you know more than you think you do." I probably had a newer version than the one written in 1946 but the message was the same, no matter which edition I had. When Lisa was born, and we found out that she had Down syndrome, I knew that Dr. Spock's book would be helpful, but I also knew that having a child with a disability would change things up a bit. As we experienced many new and different things with Lisa in our lives, I felt that there should be some kind of a brochure or book that would let parents know all the facts and answers that we had to search for and find out about by ourselves. We had some help in searching and getting the services needed, but it was a lot of information to contemplate and digest. Having a book would indeed be something that others could follow, benefit from and make life a little easier when facing the unknown while raising a child with a disability.

I knew that a reference book for people who wanted to seek

advice and get certain answers might not be possible, mainly because each state and each city has different organizations. It would be helpful but impossible to write it so all could benefit from all the information available. It would end up being more like a set of encyclopeidas, and then the information and laws would change so often that it would quickly be outdated. It took me some thirty years to write the first book about Lisa, which was more for entertainment for family and friends and less about services available. The second book I wrote about Lisa included a little more information about what parents might need to know, but I still felt that I hadn't informed the readers about some programs and organizations that would be helpful. Now I would like to at least incorporate some information that might point you in the right direction to find what you might need for yourself, a family member, a friend or an acquaintance find programs and organizations that could help. I want to touch on some of the programs and organizations that we have utilized and I must warn you, I may end up confusing you with some of the information that I am about to share with you. I have quoted a lot of sources, because of the complexity of the matter, and in doing so I hope to alleviate any chance of misrepresentation of any program in any way.

"Disability benefits are a federally run program through the Social Security Administration (SSA) to provide financial assistance to people who are disabled and unable to work. These disability benefits can help cover the costs of any medical expenses and every cost of living. Some types of benefits are the same across all states, while others may slightly, or largely differ state to state." [16]

MOUNTAINS TO CLIMB

In an earlier article, when I wrote about the Special Needs trust and the ABLE account, I mentioned SSI but I really didn't explain much about it. In fact, there are two federal programs that we have dealt with on Lisa's behalf for benefits as an adult. These programs are SSI and SSDI. "Supplemental Security Income (SSI) and Social Security Disability Insurance (SSDI) provide cash payments to people who meet the federal definition of 'disabled.' But the similarities between the two programs end there." [17]

"Although both SSI and SSDI are administered by the Social Security Administration, the two programs have vastly different financial requirements. SSI is designed to meet the basic needs of elderly, blind and disabled individuals who would otherwise have a hard time paying for food and shelter. Because SSI is narrowly tailored for this particular set of people, it has a very strict set of financial requirements, making it what is known as a 'means-tested' benefit." [18] and "SSI disability benefits are available to low-income individuals who have either never worked or who haven't earned enough work credits to qualify for SSDI." [19]

"SSDI, by contrast, is an entitlement program that is typically available to any person who has paid into the Social Security system for at least ten years, regardless of his current income and assets. (Younger beneficiaries and disabled adult children of retired or deceased workers may have to meet different requirements.) In theory, all qualified workers are potential SSDI recipients, even high-income earners." [20] "Both programs, SSI and SSDI, are overseen and managed by the Social Security Administration and the medical eligibility for disability is determined in the same manner for both programs." [21] Lisa applied for medical assistance when she was 18 and has been helped by having these benefits. "In most states, if you are an SSI beneficiary, you may be automatically eligible for Medicaid; An SSI application is also an application for Medicaid. In other states, you must apply for and establish your eligibility for Medicaid with another agency." [22]

Be aware that it varies from state to state because "your Medicaid coverage may be affected if you move from one of the 33 states that automatically grant coverage to a new state that does not. Of the states that make their own decisions regarding Medicaid coverage, seven of them use their own criteria for approval, but it is based more or less on the SSA's own criteria." [23] and "These states include: Alaska, Idaho, Kansas, Nebraska, Nevada, Oregon and Utah." [24] I wanted to mention the above, and to get it correct I had to go to different web sites to find the simplest explanation. I don't want to get all wrapped up in the details because sometimes different states offer different help. I hope that after reading this you will take the time to look into such opportunities and offers for the best information for your needs.

In searching for answers on the Medicaid program nationally, I found the following. ..."in all states, Medicaid provides coverage for some low-income people, families and children, pregnant women, the elderly, and people with disabilities. In some states, Medicaid has been expanded to cover all adults below a certain income level." [25] "Many people receive both SSI and Social Security benefits. Medicaid is linked to receipt of SSI benefits in most States. Medicare is linked to entitlement to Social Security benefits. It is possible to get both

Medicare and Medicaid." "If you get SSI and have Medicare, you will also be eligible for Extra Help with Medicare Prescription Drug Coverage without filing a separate application". [26]

According to The Health Insurance Association of America, it describes Medicaid as a "government insurance program for persons of all ages whose income and resources are insufficient to pay for health care." "As of 2013, Medicaid is a program intended for those with low income, but a low income is not the only requirement to enroll in the program. Eligibility is *categorical*—that is, to enroll one must be a member of a category defined by statute; some of these categories include low-income children below a certain wage, pregnant women, parents of Medicaid-eligible children who meet certain income requirements, and low-income seniors. The details of how each category is defined vary from state to state.

People with disabilities who do not have a work history and who receive Supplemental Security Income, or SSI, are enrolled in Medicaid as a mechanism to provide them with health insurance. Persons with a disability, including blindness or physical disability, deafness, or mental illness can apply for SSI. However, in order to be enrolled, applicants must prove that they are disabled to the point of being unable to work. In recent years, a substantial liberalization occurred in the field of individual disability income insurance, which provides benefits when an insured person is unable to work because of illness or injury." [27]

Lisa also qualifies for the Supplemental Nutrition Assistance Program (SNAP), which provides help for low-income households to buy the food needed for good health. In most states, if you receive

SSI, you may be eligible to receive SNAP assistance to purchase food. You can get such information and an application form at your local Social Security office or through the United States Department of Agriculture, Food and Nutrition Service. [28] There are some eligibility requirements and different scenarios, depending on income and other members in the household. [29] Lisa qualified because of low income. The forms that have to be filled out have a lot of questions about income, if anyone else is in the household and if there were other bills or expenses that might be a factor. The debit card that Lisa received when she first qualified cannot be used for nonfood items, heated-foods and products consumed on the premises; also, no alcohol, tobacco related products, heated foods like pizza, fried chicken in deli section, et cetera. Those who may be eligible are people who work but have a low income and those who are unemployed. There are income requirements and there is a maximum monthly income. [30]

Lisa took advantage of the Ticket to Work program that assisted her when she was trying to get a job. Help came through a vocational rehabilitation agency and Lisa was able to secure a job with the help of a job coach and a good support system throughout the process. The Ticket to Work is program is accessible through Social Security Administration. "Ticket to Work and Self Sufficiency (Ticket) program is a Federal program designed to provide Social Security disability beneficiaries the choices, opportunities and support they need to enter and maintain employment. The goal of the program is to reduce and, whenever possible, eliminate dependence on cash benefit programs." Ticket to Work also promotes increased self-sufficiency and greater independence. It is available throughout the United States. [31] You can find out more at the Social Security Administration website. [32]

In Kansas, there is also a program titled Working Healthy that is offered. Here is what I found on their website about the Working Healthy program. "Many people with disabilities want to work but worry that doing so could jeopardize their vital health and long term care coverage. Working Healthy offers people with disabilities who are working or interested in working the opportunity to get or keep Medicaid coverage while on the job. Through Working Healthy people can earn more, save more, achieve their career goals, and still maintain their health coverage. Working Healthy is a Medicaid program. To qualify for this program, a person must:

Have a disability determined by Social Security;

Be no younger than 16 and no older than 64;

Be employed (earning more than $65 per month, federal minimum wage or better, FICA withholding from wages or pay SECA if self-employed);

Have total countable income of less than 300% of the Federal poverty level;

Not be receiving Home and Community Based Services;

Not be an SSI recipient;

Not be living in a nursing facility; and

Have countable resources that are less than $15,000.

Benefits Specialists are available to discuss Working Healthy and provide benefits planning and analysis regarding the effects of earnings on cash (Social Security Disability Insurance and Supplemental Security Income) and medical benefits (Medicare and Medicaid)." [33]

There is also help from Section 8 housing, which is managed by the U.S. Department of Housing and Urban Development. Among other things, "Section 8 also authorizes a variety of 'project-based' rental assistance programs, under which the owner reserves some or all of the units in a building for low-income tenants, in return for a federal government guarantee to make up the difference between the tenant's contribution and the rent in the owner's contract with the government. A tenant who leaves a subsidized project will lose access to the project-based subsidy." [34]

With all this help for Lisa, financially, medically and for housing, I also want to share more information about some programs that encourage self-advocacy. I have always hoped that Lisa would be able to speak out for what she wanted and people would listen and then make her requests or visions happen. It doesn't always work that way, but the concept is widespread and well known. It is important that Lisa has a say in her personal life and in decisions made on her behalf. I have always wanted her to be independent, to choose the things that interest her and to know her rights and responsibilities. When I searched self-advocacy on line, I looked at The Arc organization. According to their website, "The Arc is the largest national community-based organization advocating for and serving people with intellectual and developmental disabilities and their families." Their site talks about their National Council of Self Advocates (NCSA) and is considered "a leading organization for self-advocates in The Arc and its chapter network. NCSA influences The Arc's advocacy efforts, informs The Arc's programming and ensure people with intellectual and developmental disabilities across the country have the same civil and human rights that every citizen enjoys." [35]

Because there are many local, state and national self-advocacy programs, you should look up a specific organization to find out what is available in your area. In Kansas, there are local self-advocacy chapters in the individual counties across the state and they also have a statewide advocacy group made up of adults with intellectual and/or developmental disabilities. That state program, the Self-Advocate Coalition of Kansas (SACK) "encourages and teaches people to speak up for themselves and to obtain the highest possible level of independence." Their vision statement is "that all Kansans with intellectual or developmental disabilities will have the opportunity to express opinions and make choices in order to create a life where they are treated with the same dignity and respect as persons without developmental disabilities." Their mission is "to promote empowerment and independence for adults with developmental disabilities." [36]

In Nebraska, People First of Nebraska's mission is "to empower, train, and advance advocacy so that People First and all people with disabilities are able to speak for themselves." [37] The People First of Nebraska organization also believes "that people with disabilities should be treated as equals and given the same decisions, rights, choices, responsibilities, and chances to speak up and empower themselves." [38] I have barely touched the surface of all the available services, organizations and programs that are available across the United States, but hopefully this will be enough to get you started in your quest to find the best possible options for your child's needs or that of someone you know. With any luck, this detailed and wide-ranging information didn't make you cross-eyed!

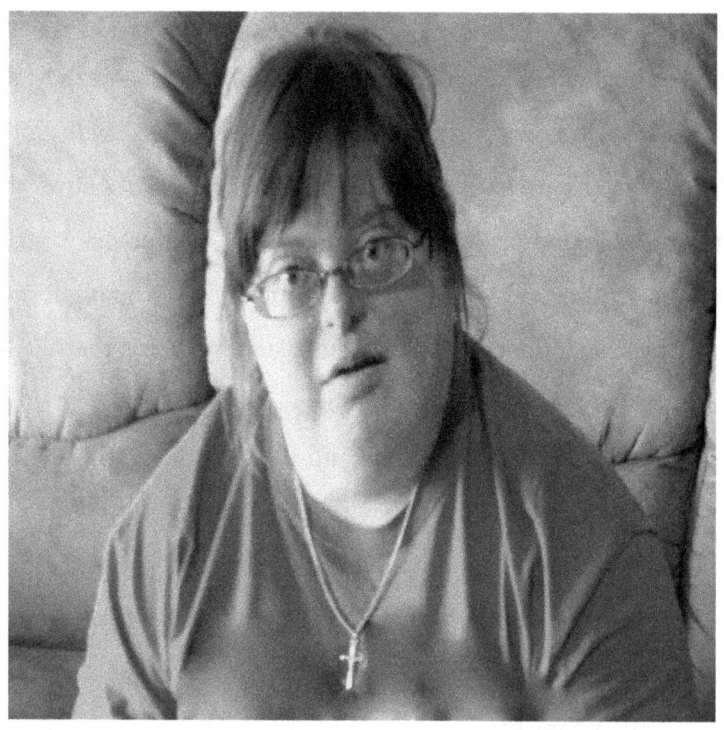

Church, Spred And Reach

Lisa had gone to church regularly when she lived at home with us, but once she moved into her own apartment she slowly chose to not attend as often. This was one of the first times that I had to restrain myself from being a mom and I gave her that option to choose. I thought to myself, "She is an adult and she can make decisions like this. I need be sure that I don't insist on her going to church with us and I need to realize that as an adult, she can and should be able to make decisions such as this." Whew, that was difficult to do. So, I just started calling her on Friday or Saturday and asking if she wanted to go with us to church on Sunday. That seemed to work out just fine.

Lisa has always been integrated into regular education in the school system and in our church activities as much as possible. She was baptized as a newborn while still in the hospital, because I was concerned about her heart situation and that she might not live long enough to have a baptism in the church. While Lisa was in grade school, she received regular religious education through our church with preparations and adjustments made for summer bible school and other church activities as available. She was always in an inclusive atmosphere and did well with the help of the other students and volunteer teachers.

When Lisa was about 16, we moved to a different state and joined a church near where we lived. This church was the same denomination as what Lisa was brought up in, so the services and prayers were the same. It was a pleasant surprise to find out that this church also offered a program for young people and adults with disabilities, to help them continue their religious education. This program was called SPRED (Special Religious Education Development) and it was designed to meet the spiritual needs of people who had a developmental or intellectual disability. There were volunteers who made a commitment to meet once a week with a curriculum that they followed. But, what I saw was less about learning and growing in the faith of our church and more about making friends and socializing. I attended a few times with Lisa so I could see what this program was about and over time I was not sure it was what we wanted for Lisa. The people who attended to learn more about the faith were people with developmental or intellectual disabilities and it was obvious there was no intention of integration with other people of the same age without disabilities. I think the SPRED program even held their sessions in a classroom somewhere else in the church hall. So, I wrote to the SPRED main office in Illinois to voice my concern. Here is part of what I wrote: "I am sure that at one time in the church, the need was there to allow those with disabilities to engage in church activities in a closed, segregated group, knowing the struggle it was for many to have their child accepted in the community. But, I am wondering if the time has come to change the format.

Why not secure volunteers who want to make a difference and have the people with disabilities join whatever religious activities are suitable, and have this same option for other young adults to take part in class time with those who have a disability. I think this would be less demeaning and more accepting than having a group of eight to ten who have a disability, all attend the same segregated church activity. If this is not possible, then at least have a new format for the SPRED program.

My challenge to SPRED is to review your goals and mission and to look at the accepting world of today. There can and should be a place for people with disabilities in today's regular bible study groups, regular religious classes and regular adult sharing organizations. No one should be thrown together simply because of their disability.

Please realize that I feel the program had its place in the past and that some still believe it is okay for their children, which is fine, but I feel it is now antiquated with today's Americans with Disabilities Act and inclusion issues. Thank you for understanding another parent's view."

Now, I realize that the SPRED program was established for people with disabilities to have a chance to learn more about their church community and I appreciate that. I just didn't like the segregation and lack of any real learning with what I saw when I was there in attendance with Lisa. I also appreciated the fact that the program encouraged others with disabilities to develop friendships, allow them to feel like they belonged and where they could share their gifts and talents. Again, my problem was that it was segregated and didn't seem to have a purpose other than to entertain those in attendance for an hour a week. I'm a tough cookie on this topic I guess. I know that part of this program did try to increase an awareness of people with disabilities in the church community, tried to include them in activities and events and attempted to use appropriate, adaptive materials with their teachings. The SPRED program was dedicated to encouraging others to grow spiritually, to receive on-going religious teachings and to allow those participants to be a part of the church community. SPRED may have changed since our experience, which happened many years ago. As it turned out, we weren't in that state more than two years, so at the next church I hoped Lisa would be able to continue with her religious education instruction in some way.

The next church had a program called REACH, which was the acronym Religious Education Program for Children with Disabilities. It struck me funny that the first program Lisa joined was called SPRED, that reminded me of people who were trying to spread and grow, trying to learn all they could about themselves and their beliefs in their church and God. And this new church program, REACH, was about the same, with people trying to reach for more, wanting to learn about their faith and wanting to do more about their principles and religious ideas. Good acronyms, I think.

REACH seemed to be a more inclusive program. This program allowed parents or a guardian to attend, to help or to sit back and listen during the hour of teaching. For some reason, I did not attend these with Lisa. Maybe it was because she was older and more confident or maybe I just thought she needed to go on her own to meet others from the church. I also felt more comfortable with this situation because when we were looking at the three churches in this town, trying to figure out which one to attend, we immediately saw that at this church's Sunday services there were noticeably more people in attendance who had a developmental disability. I felt that if the church had opened up their doors and hearts to accepting people as they are, and that those people with a disability chose to attend because they felt welcome, well then, I thought it was a good church to join. There always seems to be all kinds of barriers for people with disabilities and that shouldn't be the case when attending church. This church had some good things going for it in this regard. They had headphones for people who were hard of hearing, so that they might able to hear the service better. They had a designated service that utilized people doing sign language near the altar, so that those who were deaf would be able to follow the day's service. They had a reader who was blind, but was able to use braille to deliver the readings of the day. They had a ramp on the side of the church that connected to the front of the church, so those with wheelchairs or walkers, or those who had trouble using steps, could still enter the church through their welcoming front doors.

According to Disabilities and Faith website, the National Organization on Disability found that approximately 85% of people with and without disabilities state their religious faith is important in their lives, but only 47% of people with disabilities attend church at least once a month, most likely due to architectural, programmatic, communication and attitudinal barriers. [39] The attitudinal barriers are when people might omit others because those with disabilities may not be able to talk clearly, they are not mobile without help or they cannot behave properly around others due to their disability. Inclusion in the church setting could be encouraged by asking the parents for input and what they hope for in relationship to church involvement, trying to promote inclusion in all aspects of the church activities and services, and offer teachers the best training and assistance in teaching people with disabilities. My biggest push was to treat everyone equally, allowing all who can and are willing, to be a part of the service, classroom and other educational programs, and especially to not alienate or exclude anyone just because they have a disability.

I found the following Ten Commandments for Welcoming Persons with Disabilities to Church at the website for the Diocese of Scranton. It states:

1. Treat a person with a disability as you would anyone else. Relax when communicating. Rely on natural courtesy, consideration and common sense. Avoid getting flustered or irritated if misunderstandings arise. Repeat yourself if you sense misunderstanding, or ask the person to repeat himself or herself if you do not understand.

2. Address the individual, not an assistant, interpreter or family member.

3. Treat adults with disabilities as adults rather than as children, regardless of the disability.

4. Speak at a normal rate, without exaggeration or overemphasis.

5. Do not be afraid to ask questions about the person's disability.

6. To facilitate communication, have pads of paper and pencils available in all meeting rooms and other gathering places on parish property. Use them when helpful.

7. Allow people to do things for themselves when they want to, even if it takes longer or results in mistakes. Do not always "do for" the person.

8. Offer assistance, but do not impose if help is not desired.

9. During all gatherings or meetings, allow time to attend to personal needs and rest. Be patient.

10. Respect the individual's personal space and auxiliary aids. Do not lean against or push a wheelchair, pet a service animal in a harness, move wheelchairs, crutches, white canes or other assistive devices out of reach of a person who uses them. [40]

Having said all that, I believe the REACH program was a better fit for Lisa and for me. Lisa enjoyed a few years attending this great religious program until they finally had to discontinue the curriculum. I am glad Lisa was able to attend something so positive and rewarding with this inclusive, religious program. We still see some of the volunteers when we are in church and it's nice that Lisa knows these people in the church community and is comfortable joining in church activities. Her needs were met when we moved and joined this church and she has a positive attitude about her faith.

When Lisa and her partner, Hal were together she did not join us as often, but then she and Hal would sometimes go to his service called the Sabbath. By Jewish religious law, halakha, "Shabbat is observed from a few minutes before sunset on Friday evening until the appearance of three stars in the sky on Saturday night". [41] Lisa and Hal would get a ride from a college student and they would go to the place where the synagogue service would be held and where they would usually enjoy a meal afterwards. I was pleased that they could attend and that Lisa would be able to learn more about Hal's religion. Lisa and Hal's attendance at these services also declined over time.

For Easter Sunday one year, Lisa's dad and I, along with Lisa and Hal, were invited for an Easter Sunday church service and a meal with Lisa's brother and his family. We drove over that morning and arrived at the church, which wasn't very far away from their house. We found one long, wooden pew that would seat all eight of us and we had a few minutes before the service to sit and enjoy the joyful music sung by the choir. At one point during the service, the choir sang a powerful, uplifting and fast-paced Easter song and we all got into the rhythm and tempo of the inspiring music. Lisa was really getting into the music, moving to the beat and singing as loud as she could. She leaned over to me and said, "Mom, can I get up and dance?" Now mind you, there was no one in this church dancing, and I grew up in a conservative church where we didn't dance in church, so I didn't know what to say to her. Sadly, I told her that I didn't think so because no one else was dancing. She was okay with that answer, yet afterwards I felt that I quashed her spontaneity. She did continue to move to the beat of the music, raise her hands up and sing to her heart's content.

Another Sunday at church, our priest was singing part of the prayers of that service and the congregation would sing the response. At one point, he sang, "Let us pray," and the correct response would be to sing "Amen." Lisa was a half beat faster than the congregation and she sang in tune and on tempo, "Okay." That got a chuckle out of a few people who were sitting near us and of course giggles from Lisa's family. Lisa still attends church with us occasionally and tries to sing along with all the songs, pray the prayers and is in tune during the vocal responses. Through her actions outside of church, she shows respect for and helps others, tries to be patient and kind, and lives a life of goodness and honesty.

A New Apartment

Lisa had been living in her own apartment for a few years before she met Hal at a self-advocate, national conference. When he moved to the town where she was living, it was clear that he had an interest in her. They started seeing each other at local Parks and Recreation activities and other functions they both attended. From there, he began to visit her at her apartment, and she would go to his place on occasion. After a year or so of knowing each other, they spoke up and said they wanted to be married and live together. Well, I knew then that this would be an experience I never dreamed we would encounter and I wasn't sure how to proceed. I wasn't sure that marriage was an option but Lisa's dad and I also felt if they were serious then we should at least listen to them and try to come up with a solution that would work for them.

I was not keen on them living together, but I thought that might be a first step, so they could see if they would really be able to live together because they were both set in their ways about many issues. I finally agreed that they could try to live together but before that could happen, I had to check with Hal's parents to make sure it was agreeable with them, too. And it was! With that major concern out of the way, we began to search for a place that was suitable for both of Lisa and Hal.

At that time, Lisa's apartment had just one-bedroom and Hal was living with a roommate in another apartment complex. It was decided that they should have a two-bedroom place to give them each some space. One big issue was where they should live, his apartment complex or Lisa's. Lisa's complex was close to a grocery store but farther away from Hal's work, and he usually walked to and from work. In the end, we all agreed on an acceptable two-bedroom apartment in Lisa's complex and set to work on getting their furnishings and themselves moved over to the new place so they could begin the trial year of living together.

During that year, Lisa and Hal kept talking about getting married. After many talks with them and with Hal's mother and stepfather, it was decided a commitment ceremony was the best choice for them. It turned out to be a wonderful celebration of their love and devotion and it was what they needed to move on in their life together. Their differing abilities were apparent and as they adjusted to living together, they were able to help each other in their daily living skills. Hal had cerebral palsy that affected some fine motor skills, such as handwriting. Lisa could write, even though the process of writing is somewhat slow for her and with misspelled words. If Hal needed a note written, Lisa wrote it and Hal would help with the spelling. If Hal and Lisa went out somewhere that they might need to have some spending money, Lisa would hold on to Hal's money as well as her own. If Lisa needed to schedule a bus ride somewhere, Hal would usually do that for both of them. Hal took over a lot of the household chores, like doing the dishes, the laundry and taking out the garbage. Lisa did most of the cooking on the stove but they could both cook their meals when they used a microwave. They had their own schedules that varied slightly, but they always managed time together in the evenings, watching their favorite shows together. If they didn't agree on a show, Hal would go to his bedroom where he had his television set up, and Lisa stayed in the living room where her television was set up. They made it work for many years.

When Lisa had some mental health problems, Hal was there for emotional support. He also helped with medical issues that came up, such as the time when Lisa was having anxiety attacks and she thought they could be heart attacks. Hal called for an ambulance, and the EMTs were able to treat and reassure Lisa at their apartment. When there was a small fire on their stovetop area, Lisa was able to get the fire extinguisher and use it correctly, while Hal called an emergency line for help. Lisa extinguished the fire quickly, and then Hal and Lisa went outside to wait for the fire department. They each reacted and knew what to do in all kinds of situations and I think they handled them well.

After almost ten years together, Lisa was the one calling for help, for Hal. Before work one morning, she found Hal still in bed and he was not responding to her voice or physical shakings when she tried to wake him up. Lisa called Hal's mother, who then called an on-call number that was available for emergencies through the Supported Independent Living (SIL) agency. Lisa didn't call us, because she knew that we were vacationing out of state at the time.

Hal had died in his sleep and Lisa had reacted as best she knew how, trying to get help for Hal. The SIL staff came over immediately to be with Lisa until the ambulance arrived, and stayed while the police officers surveyed the situation and asked Lisa many questions.

One police officer noticed some photos of Lisa and some teammates of hers that showed them at a powerlifting event. That officer recognized a picture of one young man, because that young man was the son of a woman who worked at the police station. The officer called that woman to ask what she knew about Lisa, and if Lisa was capable of answering the questions he had to ask. This mother knew Lisa well enough to confirm that Lisa was capable and able to answer thoroughly, truthfully and honestly. When I was told about the staff being at the apartment for support, the police questioning Lisa and the person reaffirming that Lisa was capable, I felt relieved that she had such a great support system to help her through this ordeal. When Lisa related to me what happened that morning, she said once the staff and police were there, she didn't know what to do. I am sure she was overwhelmed with the situation and all the people who were around. Lisa told me later that she was scared and sad, and I reassured her that it was okay to be scared. I told her she did all the right things to get help for Hal and that she was very brave. I also told her that it was okay for her to be sad, because losing someone special in your life is sad. Lisa managed as well as could be expected on that day, and had help from many people. Her siblings were very supportive when they found out about Hal. After being called about the news, Lisa's sister immediately took off to drive the 5 ½ hours to be with her. Lisa's sister-in-law, who lived almost an hour away, also started the drive over to be with Lisa, but after hearing that others were headed that way to be with Lisa, this person decided to turn around and head back to her workplace. Lisa's oldest brother took off from work to drive 45 minutes from his town to where Lisa was and took her back to his place for the night. Lisa's dad and I couldn't get a flight home until the following evening, so I was so thankful for those who were able to step in and be with Lisa.

We decided that Lisa should stay with us instead of in the apartment. She settled into a new routine, but it was a difficult time for all of us. The first week was basically just going through the motions of some kind of normal, with the biggest difference being that Hal wasn't with her and that she wasn't going to any of her regular work places. After the funeral we talked to Lisa about taking some time off from work until she felt ready to go back. While Lisa was with us, we did the best we could to keep her routine as close to normal as possible. Lisa said she wanted to go back to work, because she was worried about taking too much time off or being away from her friends for too long. So, we made sure that the door-to-door bus service, the staff at her work place and other people who were involved in her weekly activities had our address so they could pick her up and get her to where she needed to be. This helped to get some normalcy back into Lisa's routine. The next step was for her to move and have an apartment of her own again. We thought a one-bedroom would be more manageable for her. We talked to Lisa about this at length and she seemed pleased with the upcoming move. One of her comments was, "I am excited to go live in the apartment. I'm not sad at all." Another time she said, "I don't feel mostly depressed but mostly happy." And later on, Lisa commented that her heart was hurting and then she would ask, "How long will it last?" After one such question, Lisa came back with a solution she thought was quite fitting. She said, "I can go hug the bear that Hal gave me." These comments made my heart swell and my tears flow because I knew she was torn between being sad because of losing Hal and trying to be happy even though she was moving on without him.

It was about eight weeks after Hal's death before we were able to get Lisa's furniture moved in and get things settled for her move from our house to her new place. Before the move, Lisa had drawn a diagram that showed where she wanted her furniture to go. Her illustration was very exact, showing the main door, marking a doorbell and a doormat in front of the door. She also drew a picture of a large heart, noting that this was "something for the door." My guess was that she wanted to decorate the front door. She marked a spot where there was a bookshelf that was secured to the wall and couldn't be moved even if we wanted it to be moved, and drew the sliding glass door that led out to a small outdoor patio. She had correctly drawn the kitchen and bedroom areas, complete with where the bed and dresser would go. The kitchen just had the entry from the dining area to the kitchen marked with a notation that she was going to have a beaded curtain that she had used in her very first apartment. Lisa marked where there would be pictures on the walls and what looked like an area rug in front of where she wanted the television to go. The framed pictures were hung on the walls but she decided not to have the rug, because there was already wall-to-wall carpet in the living room.

This was another difficult time and I was not sure I was ready for her to move out. But, I knew she needed to be out of our house because she needed to be independent again. She called us a lot at first, just to talk or to ask to go somewhere. She also realized that she had to start doing all the things that Hal had done for her, and I have to think this must have been depressing for her. He was gone and she was feeling sad and alone. Now she had to do all the chores herself. I wanted to go over there more often but I also wanted her to get comfortable being in her own place again. It was a very difficult period of time for all of us, trying to adjust to Lisa's new way of life.

Lisa started seeing a family therapist she had been to before, to help her sort out her feelings about all that had happened. I was always willing to listen, but it didn't help Lisa when I tried to talk to her about Hal because I would usually start to cry. I felt an impartial person who didn't have that closeness with Lisa and Hal might be a better fit for Lisa to talk to and the therapist knew Lisa, which helped. The therapist made up a list of things Lisa could do when she was feeling sad. Some of those suggestions included finding a place to be alone or with a supportive friend; breathe and feel your feelings; if you want to cry go ahead and cry; if it becomes painful, turn your mind to think about something happy; if the grief comes back that's ok, continue to breathe and feel the feelings. Over time, we decreased Lisa's counseling visits and then agreed that Lisa could just set up an appointment if she needed to talk with the therapist again.

In nursing school, I learned about the stages of grief and remembered a book about grieving after losing a family member. There are five stages when a person is going through the loss of a loved one. These stages are denial, anger, bargaining, depression and acceptance. We all go through the grief process at different times and we all handle those stages differently. We may not all go through all the stages or in any one certain order. We are all different and unique in our grief and sorrow. I knew Lisa would go through these stages and that it was a typical, normal process for her to do so. I tried to be patient and understanding with her and what she was going through, and I also realized that I was going through the same feelings, though obviously not in the same way. She lost her best friend, her partner, her soul mate. I couldn't imagine how that must have felt. I learned to listen, encouraged her to talk, cry and ask questions, and I knew we would get through this together, somehow. Then, I remembered a quote from Winnie the Pooh. To me, it is about knowing that you can deal with anything that might come your way. In part, the quote is "...You're braver than you believe, and stronger than you seem, and smarter than you think."

Several months later, there was a celebration of life honoring Hal. Scores of people were there and they all had a story to tell about him. It was a wonderful way to remember Hal. He was a great self-advocate and many people knew this of him. One story ended with a saying that was reportedly repeated by Hal many times. "Keep your voice heard and your chin up." After this celebration, Lisa said, "Guess what. My heart does not hurt as much anymore."

Lisa was living in her one-bedroom apartment for a while and I could tell that life without Hal was still difficult for her. Little things would come to mind and then she would be sad or teary-eyed. She talked about how scary it was when he died. Out of the blue Lisa would say something like, "I feel slammed," "This sucks" or "This is a pain in the butt," and I would ask her what she was talking about. She would then say something about Hal's death and how she didn't like what happened. I would listen and try to encourage her to talk more if she wanted, and sometimes I would try to say what I thought about the situation and how I couldn't imagine the feelings she was experiencing. I worried about her and wanted her to be able to make it on her own, as she had before she met Hal. I told her I worried about how she was feeling and how she was coping and Lisa replied quickly by saying, "Mom, you know what happens when you worry? You get warts!"

Once or twice Lisa would comment on seeing the video of Hal, and the first time she said this I asked Lisa what she meant about the video but she couldn't explain what she meant. I asked her if it was the video from the celebration of life that was held in remembrance of Hal and she would say, "No, not that." It wasn't until later on that I was informed about how some people might see a video-like replay of something tragic that had happened, as if their mind was trying to sort it all out. So, I now believe that this was what Lisa meant and it saddened me to know that she was recalling the experience over and over. I know she always felt responsible, because she couldn't save him and with each time she replayed the morning of Hal's death, she couldn't find reason or closure in the circumstance of Hal's death.

Being in her apartment was another adjustment for Lisa, with so many changes. She now had to do her own laundry, take out the trash and do the dishes. These are just some of the chores that Hal took on as his chores even though they should have also been Lisa's chores when they lived together. Lisa even asked if I would come over and help her change the sheets on her bed. Hal always did that with her. Of course I went over to help her and it gave us a chance to talk about missing Hal. We talked about the good times and special memories she had. She had recently gotten a new shower curtain and remarked that it was just like the shower curtain she had in her first one-bedroom apartment, before Hal. She said that the shower curtain was like going back to a time without Hal and that it was okay. I had not remembered that the shower curtains were so similar but Lisa did, and she found a way to believe that what had happened was as she put it, part of the circle of life, and that she could move on. When I had to leave after spending some time at the apartment with Lisa, I again felt sad that I had to leave her alone in the apartment. Just like when she was to spend her first night alone in her first apartment, I wanted to stay but now I knew that I needed to leave. I thought Lisa looked like she was going to cry, but she didn't, I did. Tears filled my eyes and I started to sniffle a little in hopes of masking the fact that I was starting to cry. Lisa told me not to cry and I said I wasn't but then I did. Lisa reached out her arms to me and hugged me and said, "I will be here if you need me."

When we got Lisa all moved in and things put away, we thought it would be good to somehow invite some of the residents in her building to come to meet Lisa, so we organized a meet and greet. It was set up for a Saturday morning with of 1 ½ hours allotted for the occasion. We had cookies and juice and I emailed some of her friends and co-workers, some of my friends who knew Lisa and the apartment residents. A few people showed up early in the time slot suggested, then others came a little later. Lisa only met one resident but to have the other people that she knew show up was a great boost for Lisa. All who attended were very upbeat and encouraging, talking so positively about Lisa, her apartment and their care and concern of Lisa. It was a nice beginning for Lisa in her new setting, and hopefully it made Lisa feel like it was her place, even if she was alone.

Lisa Speaking Out

I was calling Lisa a little more often when she moved after Hal died, and sometimes we had very little to say to each other. Lisa seemed a little uneasy with this move to a new apartment, mainly because she would be living alone and surely missing Hal. Our phone conversations hinged on what happened on that day or what she was going to do on the weekend. A staff person would take Lisa out for an hour or so and they would usually end up going to get lunch or a treat. After a few questions about what she was going to do, I would hear that they had gone to lunch. No surprise there, so at this point I would change my line of questioning.

I sometimes heard her television on in the background and asked what she was watching. Her answers were usually short and sweet. Once, I asked her if she watched any other television shows and she mentioned a couple. Then I said, "What else do you like?" and she quickly answered, "Boys." Well, I had no comeback for that answer, so again I changed the subject. Our phone conversations never last very long and most of the time we usually just stated the reason for the call, got the answer we were calling about, closed the conversation then said goodbye. Lisa has never been much of a talker, but there are times when I am pleasantly surprised by her volume, her strong voice and solid commitment when the subject is important to her.

Two of the organizations she belongs to, both local and state self-advocate programs, are very important to Lisa. She is a great self-advocate and avidly supports the programs. She helps the most when she is soliciting funds for a chili feed or a pancake feed that are big fundraisers for these organizations. I have been on the other end of the phone when Lisa calls us to ask for help in supporting these worthy causes. She usually calls us about ten minutes after she has gotten home from one of their meetings that might have just been a preliminary start in the members trying to discuss and organize for the next event. Lisa may not even know the date or time, and possibly not even the place, but she would want us to know what little she knew, so we can buy tickets to attend or donate money if we can't make it. Her 'spiel' is always very polite and to the point.

I have heard from Lisa's siblings, aunts and uncles, and some of our friends about her very straightforward approach to asking for money or help. And, if the person she called didn't answer their phone, she would leave a detailed message, noting the cost of tickets or suggesting a higher amount if they couldn't attend, donating money and tickets so someone else could attend. It is always amazing to me and to others she has talked to, about how well she does relaying the information because Lisa is basically a quiet and reserved person when she talks. But give her a program that involves her and her beliefs, and she is all over it.

She will also speak up at meetings that she has attended with her dad and I. The Arc has annual meetings with an agenda that includes voting for items of concern, hearing about who is on the board or sharing about the year in review. A guest speaker is included in the meeting and is usually someone who is knowledgeable in the field of ID/DD (intellectual disabilities/developmental disabilities) issues and the ongoing needs. It never fails that Lisa would raise her hand to ask a question. When Lisa first started attending such meetings, I would try to get Lisa's attention, shake my head "no" or whisper to Lisa that she could wait and ask me later instead of taking up time during the meeting. (What was I thinking?) Lisa had a right to ask questions just the same as any other person attending that meeting. Lisa was able to ask her questions and I soon realized that her questions were pertinent, well thought out and sometimes made the speaker think because of the weight of Lisa's questions. The speaker would answer with a sensible, satisfying and sincere response. So, I quickly gave up trying to prohibit Lisa from asking questions and I just tried to sit back, listen to the speaker and wait for Lisa to come up with a question that needed to be asked and answered. If Lisa were not there in attendance, those questions might not have been asked. I am reminded of a line from the movie, Wonder; "You can't blend in when you were born to stand out." I think that includes Lisa.

More recently, during a yearly update required by the state to see if Lisa progressed in her daily living skills as well as if she had any changes in her mental or physical status, Lisa voiced a possible measurable goal, which was to be a better advocate for herself and others. She mentioned that she could go to more meetings and be more involved in order to support her goal. She also voiced a concern that she would like people to listen or pay attention to her when she talks. There was discussion about this goal that was helpful and those in attendance that day encouraged Lisa while they mentioned some helpful words of wisdom in addition to her going to more meetings. They said things like, "If you would just talk a little louder," or "You might try to speak clearly and not mumble," or "You could get their attention and maintain eye contact." I followed up those comments with a reminder that what they had just suggested has been on Lisa's IEP from the time she was little. I wasn't sure it would be that simple for Lisa. Then Lisa responded with her own suggestion. She loudly replied that what she needed was a gavel. She continued by saying she could pound it on a table and get everyone's attention. This made us all grin as we tried to contain our giggles. Before the meeting was over, Lisa added that she would like to have her nickname changed. Well, this was news to me, because I didn't know she had a nickname. In her best voice, she told us that she would now like to be known as The Hammer.

Lisa also loves to talk when there is a mike in her hand. When she participated in her twice a year play productions through our parks and recreation program, there was a time when the actors and actresses would be recognized at the end of the curtain calls. Each participant would receive a flower and take their individual bow. Some bows lasted longer and were more energetic than others, but they would take the time for this special ending. Usually, the person in charge who was calling each individual to the front of the stage had the mike. That person would always say a few kind words to the parents, friends or others who might be in the audience. Sometimes individual actors would reach for the mike to say a few words, too. But, when everyone who was a part of the play started taking the mike, it went on for at least another half hour or so after the bows.

A few times Lisa was able to say a few words and she always spoke up, was to the point, took her well thought out bow and left the stage beaming. After one stage production finale, some time after Hal died, I got teary eyed and was so proud of her. She met us after the show, reached out to give me a big bear hug and said, "I couldn't have done this without you."

Looking Through My Glasses

The following book of poetry, Looking Through My Glasses, was written and illustrated by Lisa. When she asked if it could be published, I agreed to help her. Lisa and I discussed how to compile the book, and I received permission from her to alter her original drafts by correcting some spelling errors. Other than that, I have kept her written words as close to the original as possible. Lisa has been a major force in this decision-making process. She is inspirational to me and I hope she is to others throughout her lifetime. For thirty years, I've been known as "Lisa's mom," and happily, I always will be.
      Angee Barcus
      January 2010

Shapes and Colors All Around

Spooker, my cat, is white like a diamond and different shapes.
Grapefruit is tart and sweet and nutritious.
Sun shines like a stone and turns bright pink at night.
Diet coke tastes more like cement.
Candles glow so bright, the whole room lights up.
Bunnies are cute with them hopping on
Easter day as the church appears.

To the Season be Jolly!

Holidays, Holidays are loving, giving and caring.
Important time of the year when Christmas is near.
Fa la, Fa La to be jolly to the season.
Bound to the season to be jolly, Fa la, Fa la.
Now you see and hear the day of caroling;
Fa la, Fa la to the season to be jolly.

Winter Thoughts

Roses are red, roses are blue; Sugar is sweet and so are you.
Can it be true? Christmas is near and time for Jack Frost;
He is nibbling at your nose when the wind beneath you
and you can see it.
Church bells are ringing, ring ding, ring ding.
Church bells are ringing.
Peace out! Yeah.

Valentine's Day

Valentine's Day is an imposition;
On this holiday, which is so boring when,
I have no one to celebrate with.
What's up with that, but they speed it along; what's up with that?

March Thoughts

March is my favorite month around.
When St. Patrick's Day and springtime is near;
soon our one-year anniversary is near.
Run around in green grass; hide Easter eggs for kids to find.
Maybe going fishing or grilling out, watching evening butterflies.

That's My Baby

I miss my baby. I miss the way we joke around.
I miss going romantic and music; I love him like crazy.
I miss that he tucks me in to bed and kisses me goodnight.
I miss his snacks at night. I miss his stories at night.
I love him the way he does himself.
I love him when he gives me candy and soda pop.
I love that he wakes me up every morning. That's my baby.

I'd Be Surprised

I'd be surprised if my baby is back.
I'd be surprised if he got back early.
I'd be surprised if he tells me all about his trip.
I'd be surprised to actually see my baby.
I'd be surprised if my baby got me something.
I'd be surprised if my baby gives me $4 for pop; I'd be surprised.
I'd be surprised if only my baby were back in my arms.

Roses in Colors

Roses are red, roses are blue; sugar is sweet and so are you.
Can it be true? I love you.
Roses are orange, roses are yellow; sugar is sweet and so are you.
Can it be true? You're my honey.
Roses are black, roses are purple; sugar is sweet and so are you.
Can it be true? You're my sugar lips.
Roses are red, roses are blue; sugar is sweet and so are you.
Can it be true? You're my honey bear.

Our Anniversary

Over the past two years the sun rises on our anniversary.
I love you forever.
You are the flower in my heart.

Advocacy, Advocacy

We stand up for our rights. Make our voices heard.
Advocacy, Advocacy
We know our rights. We know our responsibilities.
Advocacy, Advocacy
It is to have fun and dance.
Advocacy, Advocacy
It is for us to learn within the entire nation.

Flowers and Me

Each flower tells a story;
I see they are like me, special toes, made like a new crown,
I am like you, new rose, just like you with a token of my love,
Like I was a child in you.

Food Thoughts

Trees; all shapes within sizes; some have fruit upon them.
Palm trees have coconuts; one drops upon the head, clinks,
rocks, even on shoulders.
Roast pig with red meat might look good with vegetables.
Cake, cupcakes, baked glass even under glass; have you tasted it?

Junk Food

Junk food is bad for you.
Once in a while you can eat a big meal,
but never too much
or you'll get fat or bigger.

My Grandma

My Grandma, my Grandma; she shines like a diamond around me,
gives surprises and goodies.
She fixes my hair like an ocean, wavy and rocky;
she feels light, like a feather.
That float she used to float when she's celebrating life.
With Thanksgiving upon us, she gave the words
"I will come to the wedding day."
Now she sank like two rocks; she died.

Happy Moments

My Grandma, my Grandma;
She might be old but is a best friend I ever had.
She goes and has a good time; took me out fishing, horseback riding;
What happy moments.

Boys

Boys are sweet sometimes.
They are flattering, some are not.
Some are different.
Lisa is sweet in some ways and hard at first.

My Mom

Mom is my friend, the best friend.
Mom is mom; she wants me be healthy, exercise daily.
Mom is mom; she helped me to grow up right.
Mom is mom; she loves me how I am.
Mom is mom; what a friend she is.

A School Thought

Theology is about what we learn about in homework
or different seeing of our vision that is different.
Some are different than others.

School Help

We need help sometimes with reading or writing or spelling;
It is how we become better writers.

Obesity

Obesity I hate.
Obesity sucks big time.
I get teased, and have low self-esteem.
Obesity kills more people and children.

Stress

Over the past two years I have had an overload
of work and a lot of stress. I'm just one person.
(Written in 2010)

Night Show

Lighting,
Bright like a star glows as light;
Puts on a good show;
Really neat angle like a shooting star.

The Blooming Flowers

Flowers bloom for joy,
Flowers bloom for love,
Flowers bloom for happy,
Flowers bloom even when you're feeling sad.

Spooky Night

The power is off.
What fun, but it is spooky at night, when the power comes on;
it's even prettier.

Differences

With people with disabilities, we are different.
In some ways, there are learning disabilities, some are not.
There are some as brain damage or autism.
So many ways; <u>never give up hope</u>,
or thoughts and dreams on kids like us.
We can't read or talk, kids with developmental disabilities.
We are smart not dumb.
We can learn with or without your help.

Downs' Syndrome

My hands are not contagious.
I have Downs' syndrome; and I have a special line
in the middle that is called a simian line.
You might see us as retarded because we can't learn on our own;
We are smart, and never give up or hate. We can learn.
If we need help we will ask the teachers for our homework;
We will have the glasses we need in the world.

The Visitor

This final story is the end of the book but not the end of Lisa's stories. There are many more adventures that will come our way with Lisa in our lives. We anticipate the joys we will experience, while watching Lisa as she continues to mature and develop in the coming years. This final story is actually from the beginning of Lisa's life, when she was just a newborn baby, all cute, cuddly and huggable. Over the years, I have only shared this story with a few people, such as Lisa's dad and a few friends from church but I feel this is the best way to end this book, by starting at the beginning.

I was thrilled to hear we had a girl when Lisa was born, but the excitement soon ended when I found out she had some problems. The words Down syndrome confused me. The doctor clarified that diagnosis by using outdated terms such as retarded and mongoloid. I was scared. I could not believe this could happen to us. How would we take care of a child with a disability? I cried about our precious Lisa; her future seemingly wiped away. As it turned out, Lisa did have a future and it has been good. With all the trials of raising a child with a disability and with all the health problems that Lisa has experienced, I believe my ability to cope came from a stranger who entered our house in the middle of the night, to deliver the words that I may not have always believed but that I will always remember.

When Lisa was born, I was the one who cried. My husband was struggling to cope with the unanticipated situation, but he seemed to hold it together, being very supportive and understanding of my overwhelming emotions. He would look at Lisa and say "That's too bad," but he seemed to be able to get around this unexpected diagnosis. I, on the other hand, cried when I saw her, I cried when I held her, I cried when I thought about all the things I wanted for her that I thought would never happen. Then, I cried even more when the doctors gave us worse news. Yes, I say worse, because once I heard the latest findings in Lisa's newborn check-up, her having Down syndrome did not seem to be as critical.

Doctors noticed Lisa had some type of congenital heart condition, suspecting at least one hole in her heart. We would not learn of the severity until we could take her into a pediatric cardiologist later in the week. It was definitely obvious she had heart problems because she would become dusky and blue in color. Now, I worried about her dying in my arms. I cried about her health and her uncertain future. Would she live? I had also been praying that this diagnosis of Down syndrome was a mistake. A chromosome test was done that would prove or disprove the diagnosis. Until that chromosome test result was made known, I pretended not to see the obvious signs, and prayed that the doctors were wrong.

There was no denying the outward signs; slanted eyes, small, low-set ears, the simian lines on the palms of her hands, and now the heart problem, which is common in children with Down syndrome. I whispered some bargaining prayers to God, asking that he take care of the heart problems, and that I would be able to deal with the Down syndrome. Yet, each time Lisa turned dusky and blue, I felt my prayers were not being answered in the way I thought they should. During the four days Lisa and I stayed at the hospital, my time was filled with getting to know Lisa, caring for her, loving her and praying.

On our first night at home, I was very nervous with Lisa. That seems rather silly to me now, since we'd had three other children, brought them home from the hospital, and loved and cared for the newest member without hesitation or trepidation. But, with Lisa, the health issues, and the idea of raising someone with Down syndrome were on my mind. I worried that she might die before we could get her to the specialist, so we kept her close to us at nighttime, having her bassinet next to our bed. I'm not sure that my thinking was clear, because in looking back, I wonder what I could have done. Just having her next to us wouldn't stop the seemingly inevitable, but for me it gave me some comfort having her close.

It was on this first night home from the hospital, after my husband and I had gotten the other children up to bed, that we had an unexpected occurrence. I had finished giving Lisa her bottle, did her diaper change, and got into bed. Our bedroom was on the first floor of this 100-year old house. The room opened up into the living room and when we bought the house, the only sign of a door was a heavy, worsted wool damask curtain that hung on a large, wooden dowel. Both were probably as old as the house. We had recently taken those curtains down and added glass-paned French doors.

They gave us a little more privacy and added a nice old-world charm to the house. The doors were slightly ajar, so I could hear the other children during the night if they should happen to get up.

I had quickly fallen into a deep sleep. It wasn't very long before I was suddenly sitting up in bed, not knowing what woke me. What happened next was something I have only repeated to a few chosen people. My husband was not awake for this, even though he was lying right next to me in bed. I looked towards the doors and I saw a person standing on the other side, in the living room area. To this day, I don't know if it was a male or female, and I didn't ever see the face of this person.

This person was dressed in a long, floor length white robe that flowed and softly swished with any movement. I can't say that I even saw this person walk, because when this person moved closer to our bedroom doors and to me, it was more like a gliding or smooth movement, not like that of someone who was taking individual steps. I saw this person move quickly to the side of the bassinet and laid a hand on Lisa. Then just as quickly, the person turned to me and began to speak. I was fully aware that I didn't hear the words with my ears, but somehow heard the words just then same, in my heart. What this individual said was "Don't worry about her. She'll be okay." I was not scared, but curious as to what was happening. I never uttered a word of concern, nor did this person explain their presence that night.

I know those are the words, just exactly as they were spoken. Nothing more, nothing less. I looked at the bassinet, and then back to the place where that person had been standing. All I saw was a quick movement at the bedroom doors and something in white swiftly retreating away into the dark living room. That person was there one second and gone the next. The entire episode may have taken all of two minutes. I remained sitting up in bed, looking around, to be sure I wasn't dreaming. It happened so fast and quietly that my husband did not wake up.

I thought about the incident the next morning, when we got Lisa ready to go to the pediatric cardiologist. I would recall the encounter any time I started to worry about Lisa and situations concerning her that I really had no control over. Yet, because I wore my emotions on my sleeve, I did worry. I would then feel bad, because I thought I did not have the kind of faith that would allow me to just take things as they happened and not worry so much.

Those seven simple words did not haunt me. They gave me comfort that someone else was in control and things would turn out okay. Yet, throughout Lisa's lifetime, there have been certain instances where I did worry, as any mother would. I worried when she had her first heart catherization, her first hospital stay and her first surgery. Other firsts that weren't health related but still a concern for me were things like her first time being taken by van to her pre-school, her first time in a fully inclusive educational setting with her peers and her first time swimming, riding a bike or learning another new skill.

These milestones brought me great joy and apprehension. Watching Lisa trying new things without a hint of concern made me think she was too naïve to know how the "real" world would treat her, yet she continued to do every thing she could, and she always did her best. My husband always says that Lisa is the bravest person he knows. This is because she has to be taught to do things that other children could master on their own. Then, after being taught something, she is challenged to do the next activity, the next skill level that is expected or the next hurdle to get over. She never complains. She is also put in situations that would be scary for anyone, yet she masters each situation, powers through and is now a contributing adult in the real world.

I would occasionally think back to that first night when she was brought home from the hospital, and the stranger who told me these words, "Don't worry about her. She'll be okay." Now, after all these years I wonder if Lisa knew something I didn't? Was she able to take things in stride better than me? Had she known all along that she could do anything she set her mind to, because she had an unknown source of help and encouragement?

"Don't worry about her. She'll be okay." I will never forget those words. I don't know who this person was who visited me that evening and I don't need to know. After all these years, I have come to believe that what was said that night was from either an angel or God himself. I have also tried to do less worrying, as I know that "she'll be okay," just as I was told by the nighttime visitor so many, many years ago.

If you have enjoyed this book, I would appreciate any feedback you may have. You may reach me at abBooks3@gmail.com. All comments or suggestions are welcome. I would also appreciate it if you would please take a few minutes to leave a book review on-line at https://www.amazon.com. Your honest, positive reviews will help me to reach many more readers.

Reference list

Section 8 Housing
P. 3 [1] https://en.wikipedia.org/wiki/Section_8_(housing)

Special Olympics
P. 16 [2] www.specialolympics.org
Then look under What We Do

Atlantoaxial Instability
P. 17 [3] https://www.healthychildren.org
Then search for Atlantoaxial instability

Atlantoaxial Instability
P. 17 [4] https://www.ndsccenter.org/?s=atlantoaxial+instability

Sjogren's
P. 107 [5] https://www.mayoclinic.org/diseases-conditions/sjogrens-syndrome/symptoms-causes/syc-20353216

Dry Mouth
P. 110 [6] https://www.medicinenet.com/dry_mouth/article.htm#what_is_dry_mouth

Alzheimer's and Dementia
P. 136 [7] https://www.alz.org/alzheimers_disease_steps_to_diagnosis.asp
Paragraph 3 Web site: Alzheimer's association

Abilify
P. 137 [8] https://www.webmd.com/drugs/2/drug-64439-4274/abilify/details

EKG
P. 149 [9] https://www.webmd.com/heart-disease/electrocardiogram-ekgs#1

Oral Language Modification (OLM)
P. 156 [10] http://www.safedrivingforlife.info/blog/disability-and-theory-test

Driving
P. 157 [11] http://www.safedrivingforlife.info/blog/disability-and-theory-test

Special Needs Trusts
P. 169 [12] http://www.margolis.com/Our-Blog/bid/90599/What-s-the-Difference-Between-Supplemental-and-Special-Needs-Trusts-Massachusetts.com

ABLE Account
P. 172 [13] http://www.ablenrc.org/about/what-are-able-accounts

ABLE Account
P. 173 [14] www.ablenrc.org

Special Needs Trusts
P. 173 [15] https://estate.findlaw.com/trusts/special-needs-trusts-faq-s.html

Disability Benefits
P. 176 [16] https://www.disability-benefits-help.org/faq/disability-states

SSI and SSDI
P. 177 [17] https://www.specialneedsanswers.com

SSI and SSDI
P. 177 [18] https://www.specialneedsanswers.com
Then search SSI and SSDI

SSI and SSDI
P. 177 [19] https://www.disabilitysecrets.com
Then search SSDI & SSI

SSI and SSDI
P. 177 [20] https://www.specialneedsanswers.com

SSI and SSDI
P. 178 [21] https://www.disabilitysecrets.com

What is SSI
P. 178 [22] https://www.ssa.gov/ssi/

Medicaid Coverage
P. 178 [23] https://www.disability-benefits-help.org/faq/disability-states

Medicaid Information
P. 178 [24] https://www.medicaid.gov

Health and Human Services
P. 178 [25] https://www.hhs.gov/answers/index.html
Then search for Who Is Eligible For Medicaid

SSI and Social Security benefits
P. 179 [26] https://www.ssa.gov

Medicaid
P. 179 [27] https://en.wikipedia.org/wiki/Medicaid

SNAP information
P. 180 [28] https://www.ssa.gov/pubs/EN-05-10101.pdf

SNAP
P. 180 [29] https://www.fns.usda.gov/snap/snap-application-and-local-office-locators

SNAP- Food Topics
P. 180 [30] https://www.fns.usda.gov

Ticket To Work
P. 181 [31] https://www.yourtickettowork.ssa.gov

SSA and Ticket To Work
P. 181 [32] https://www.ssa.gov Then search for Ticket To Work

Working Healthy
P. 182 [33] http://www.kdheks.gov/hcf/workinghealthy/

Section 8 Housing
P. 182 [34] https://en.wikipedia.org/wiki/Section_8_(housing)

National Council of Self Advocates (NCSA)
P. 183 [35] www.thearc.org

Self-Advocate Coalition of Kansas (SACK)
P. 183 #36 www.sackonline.org

People First
P. 183 #37 http://www.peoplefirstnebraska.com/mission.html
Then search for Mission

People First
P. 183 #38 http://www.peoplefirstnebraska.com/about.html
Then search for About

Disabilities and Faith
P. 189 #39 www.disabilitiesandfaith.org

Ten Commandments for Welcoming Persons
P. 191 #40 www.dioceseofscranton.org/parish-life-and-evangelization/ministry-with persons-with -disabilities/

Shabbat
P. 191 #41 https://en.wikipedia.org/wiki/Shabbat

Resources

The Arc-For People with Intellectual and Developmental Disabilities   http://www.thearc.org

The Arc of Nebraska 3601 Calvert St Ste 25
Lincoln, NE 68506-5797
Website: www.arc-nebraska.org
Facebook: https://www.facebook.com/pages/The-Arc-of-Nebraska/167646211703
Phone: (402) 475-4407
Email: Edison@arc-nebraska.org

The Arc of Douglas County
2518 Ridge Ct Ste 238
Lawrence, KS 66046-4061
Website: www.thearcdcks.org
Facebook: https://www.facebook.com/pages/The-Arc-of-Douglas-County/208030402553129
Business Phone: (785) 749-0121
Chapter Email: bbishop@thearcdcks.org
Chapter #: 594

National Down Syndrome Society, 666 Broadway, 8th Floor,
New York, New York, 10012
http://www.ndss.org   1-800-221-4602

National Down Syndrome Congress
30 Mansell Court, Suite 108
Roswell, GA 30076
Toll free, at 1-800-232-NDSC (6372), Monday though Friday from 9:00 AM to 5:30 PM eastern time.

National Association for Down Syndrome
http://www.nads.org
1460 Renaissance Drive
Suite #405
Park Ridge, IL 60068
1-630-325-9112

Down Syndrome Guild of Greater Kansas City
http://www.kcdsg.org
5960 Dearborn St #100, Mission, KS 66202Phone:(913) 384-4848

About the Author

Mountains to Climb: Lisa and Down Syndrome Challenges covers personal health issues and programs available that might be relevant to other children and their families. Angee Barcus includes stories about Lisa's independence, how Lisa moved out to live on her own in the community and some encouraging stories involving Lisa's strength, determination and perseverance.

Mountains to Climb concludes a sequence of books about Lisa. With encouragement from others, Angee has fulfilled a personal goal of sharing with others what she has learned about raising a child with Down syndrome. Angee's hope is that she has made a difference in the lives of other people who are on a journey through similar situations as Lisa and her family have experienced.

Angee is a wife, mother and writer. She loves to read, and writing helps her to sort out issues that might otherwise fester and linger. She is grateful for the opportunity to share her experiences. For Angee, writing and sharing are tools to help others. Angee wrote a newspaper column for almost two years and enlightened others about disability issues in and around where she lived, alternating those articles with short stories about Lisa.

Her nursing career allowed her to work in a school system, helping young children with developmental disabilities. This gave Angee another viewpoint about children with disabilities, which helped her when writing about Lisa.

Angee has written two other books, *Snapshots Of Lisa: A Candid Look At Down Syndrome And Snippets Of Lisa's Life* and *Loving And Learning: Life With Lisa And Down Syndrome*. They also relate to Lisa's life starting from birth up to her high school years. Now that the books are in print, Angee will enjoy playing the piano and the accordion more often, as well as trying to finish a few quilting and sewing projects.